ULTIMATE AIR FRYER BAKING

ULTIMATE AIR FRYER BAKING

OVER 80 DELICIOUS SWEET & SAVOURY BAKES

Dominique Eloïse Alexander & Izy Hossack

CONTENTS

INTRODUCTION

We first met on a photo shoot in the early days of our careers, with Izy taking the pictures and Dom styling the food and the props. We soon realized that our styles matched perfectly and that we had a shared passion for baking.

Years later, after Izy begrudgingly bought an air fryer for work (it's not uncommon for food stylists to get annoyed by having to own so many kitchen gadgets!), she quickly became obsessed with using it. She found it especially good for baking small-batch desserts, as it's essentially a tiny convection oven, and shared this info with Dom, another recent air fryer convert.

Together we decided to write this book, filled with deliciously achievable bakes and tips for baking in an air fryer. In the following chapters you'll find an array of sweet and savoury recipes, from casual bakes you can mix up quickly to more impressive desserts that are perfect for sharing.

AIR FRYER ANATOMY

The air fryer has quickly become a must-have in the kitchen, so let's start with understanding exactly what it is and how you can use it to create beautiful bakes.

Essentially an air fryer is a table-top convection oven with a strong fan that helps the hot air circulate throughout the drawer, cooking your food evenly. There are four main parts of an air fryer: the top-down heating element, the high-speed fan, the perforated crisper plate and the cooking drawer (also sometimes known as the basket).

The Crisper Plate

The crisper plate elevates whatever you're cooking off the base of the drawer and allows this hot air to circulate. It can be removed – helpful for cleaning and certain recipes.

The Controls

The controls may be on the front or the top of your air fryer. You may need to play around with the settings to get the temperature required in a recipe – some air fryers only allow low temperatures on 'dehydrate' mode, for example.

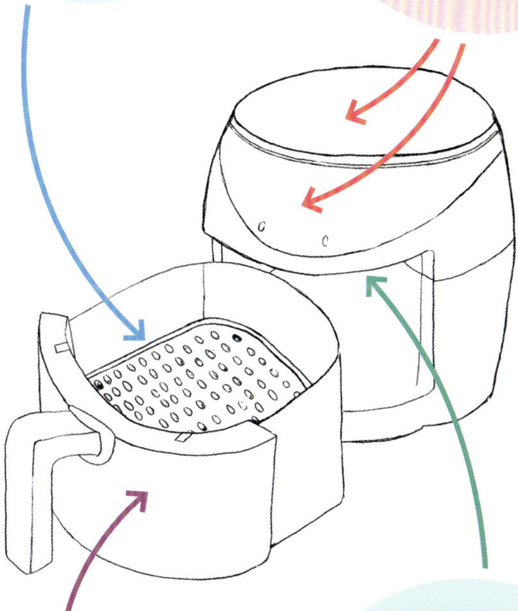

The Cooking Drawer

The cooking drawer, in its various shapes and sizes, is the main area for cooking and is what you'll need to measure to ensure your cake tins fit.

The Top-Down Heating Element

The top-down heating element is like a grill in your oven, except this one can be precisely programmed with its temperature. The fan, in conjunction, helps to rapidly blow the hot air around the drawer to provide an all-around bake.

TIPS FOR AIR FRYER BAKING

Choosing your air fryer

We've tested all the recipes in the two most popular brands' large-capacity air fryers - the Ninja Max Pro AF140 4.7L and the Cosori Pro 4.7L. They feature a large, square single drawer with a crisper plate, as well as a wide range of temperatures (from around 75°C/170°F to 240°C/465°F). We have also tested numerous recipes in dual drawer air fryers to ensure even baking across the board.

We noticed that the Ninja had a stronger fan which, for delicate bakes and liquids, created a slight vortex and/or caused peaks in the centre of bakes, whereas the Cosori's more gentle approach allowed bakes time to set without the need to cover them earlier in the bake time. We really recommend covering bakes to ensure that the top-down heat doesn't burn them and to prevent peaking, so take the advice in the recipes as needed to work with your air fryer.

If you have a dual drawer air fryer, you may need to bake things in batches or in slightly smaller tins or muffin cases. This will change the bake times, so be aware that you'll need to start checking for doneness earlier than the recipe may state. Use other recipes in the book for the size tin you're using as a guide, as well as our basic Sponge Cake on page 14 for reference.

Getting an even bake

As the air fryer bakes from a top-down heating element, it can take longer for bakes to cook all the way through and for the bottom of them to get crispy or set. For this reason, we sometimes recommend turning your bakes over to ensure even cooking.

This also means that the heat is quite intense in the first few minutes of baking, so levelling out your cakes is really important as the batters don't have time in an air fryer to slowly even out. You can use the back of a spoon or palette knife to do this.

When baking with liners (silicone or parchment), if you find your bakes aren't crisping up well enough, try removing the liner in the last few minutes and baking directly on the crisper plate if you can.

If you find the top of your bake is browning too quickly, you can cover it tightly with foil or with the bottom of a larger loose-bottomed cake tin part-way through baking, to prevent it from burning.

OTHER BAKING TIPS

- Always turn off your air fryer at the socket after you've finished baking.
- Ensure you follow the manufacturer's directions on how far away from the wall the air fryer needs to be and make sure it's placed on a heatproof surface during use.
- Use fully metal binder clips to secure the sides of your baking paper when baking in square tins or loaf tins. If you don't clip it to the edges of the tin, the baking paper can fall into your bake and squash it!
- Be careful with the height of your baking paper, too - if it's too tall or not clipped down, it could catch on the heating element.
- If your crisper plate has a handle in the middle of it and it's making your tins wobbly, trying flipping the crisper plate over so that its surface is completely flat.

KEY EQUIPMENT

Metal cake tins

Based on the air fryers we used for writing these recipes, we found that using 18 or 20 cm (7 or 8 inch) round cake tins worked best. You could also use 15 or 18 cm (6 or 7 inch) square tins, as long as you avoid those with a wide rim, as this can make them slightly too large to fit in the air fryer. For loaf cakes, a 450 g (1 lb) loaf tin is the perfect size to fit in the drawer.

Cupcake/muffin cases

Silicone versions are great for the air fryer, as they maintain their shape without requiring a muffin pan to sit them in. If you're using paper cases, you'll need to place each one in a ramekin before filling with batter, otherwise they'll flatten during baking.

Ceramic or enamel baking dishes

For some recipes where you're scooping the dessert straight out of the dish it's baked in, we like using 15 or 18 cm (6 or 7 inch) round or square ceramic or enamel dishes. They are ideal for anything with a liquidy filling, like a crumble, as they will hold in all the juices (unlike a loose-bottomed cake tin!).

Binder clips (fully metal)

We use binder clips to secure baking paper to the top edges of square cake tins. This stops the baking paper flapping around in the air fryer – if left to flap, it can fall into your bakes, deforming them. The binder clips also prevent the baking paper from flapping up and hitting the heating element, which can cause it to burn. Just make sure to buy clips that are fully made of metal, as they need to be able to survive the heat of the air fryer.

Ramekins

These can be useful for supporting paper cupcake cases to stop them collapsing. They're also perfect for individual bakes, like our Apple Crumble for One and Sticky Toffee Pudding for One (see pages 70 and 78). We go for the 225 g (8 oz) ramekins for these, as they provide ample room for batters to rise without overflowing.

Baking paper, foil and parchment liners

We often use a square of baking paper to line the crisper plate of the air fryer when baking things like cookies. For the Single Chocolate Chip Cookie recipe (see page 72), we found using a square of kitchen foil to line the crisper plate worked better, because baking paper tended to flap around and deform the cookie. You can buy pre-cut parchment liners for your air fryer, which are nice for hassle-free prep. You can also DIY a parchment liner by cutting a piece of baking paper which is larger than your air fryer drawer, scrunching it up into a ball, unfolding it and then pressing it into the drawer.

INGREDIENTS

All ingredients are as stated in the recipe. It is important to weigh ingredients for accuracy as is always the case in baking, but particularly for these recipes as they are generally small-batch bakes and so the margin for error is smaller. For example, egg sizes must be used as stated (medium and large) as the liquid in a larger egg might make your mixes too runny and not bake correctly.

1

THE BASICS

These are our air fryer versions of the key building blocks of bakes! They will be helpful for other recipes in the book and provide great starting points for you to create air fryer bakes of your own.

SPONGE CAKE

Prep time . . . . . 15 minutes

For the Sponge

120 g (4 oz) . . . . . butter or margarine, softened
120 g (4 oz) . . . . . caster/soft light brown sugar
1 tablespoon . . . . vanilla extract or paste (optional)
2. . . . . medium eggs
150g (5½ oz) . . . . self-raising flour (you can replace 30 g/1 oz with unsweetened cocoa powder to make a chocolate sponge) or you can use 150g (5½ oz) plain flour + 1½ teaspoons baking powder
splash . . . . milk

1. Add the softened butter or margarine and sugar to a mixing bowl and either beat by hand or use a hand mixer until they get light and fluffy. Stir in the vanilla, if using.
2. Crack in the eggs and beat well before adding in the flour in 2 parts, folding to mix each time. Then add the splash of milk and mix until smooth.
3. Add to your chosen cake tin or case (see right) and level out well.
4. Air fry as directed right.

This sponge recipe can be used to make all sorts of delicious cakes and, depending on your cake tin and air fryer sizes, we've provided bake times and details below so you get the best results. This can be used as a reference for most of the cake recipes in the book, so use it to make your cakes work for the kit you have. You will also know your air fryer best, so if you know it runs hot, cover the cakes with foil a little earlier. The best way to test if something is baked through is to poke a cocktail stick in the centre - it should come out with just a couple of crumbs on it. You can also get creative with add-ins and icings to make up your own recipes, so take this as a starting point and have fun!

SUGGESTED BAKE TIMES

• 15 and 18 cm (6 and 7 inch) round tin:

Temperature: 160°C (325°F)
Bake: 20 minutes uncovered, then 30–35 with foil over the top
Serves: 6–8

• 15 and 18 cm (6 and 7 inch) square tin:

Temperature: 160°C (325°F)
Bake: 20 minutes uncovered, then 20–23 with foil over the top
Serves: 9

• 6 x 175 ml (6 fl oz) muffins/ cupcakes (large):

Temperature: 160°C (325°F)
Bake: each silicone or cupcake case in a ramekin: 10 minutes, then turn ramekin 180 degrees, 7 more minutes
Serves: 6

• 12 x 75 ml (2½ fl oz) fairy cakes (small):

Temperature: 150°C (300°F)
Bake: each silicone or cupcake case in a ramekin: 10 minutes, then turn ramekin 180 degrees, 7–8 more minutes
Serves: 12

• 450g (1lb) loaf tin:

Temperature: 160°C (325°F)
Bake: 25 minutes uncovered, then 35 minutes with foil over the top
Makes: 6–8 slices

• 18-20 cm (7-8 inch) bundt tin:

Temperature: 160°C (325°F)
Bake: 20-25 minutes
Serves: 10-12

BASIC BUTTERCREAM

Makes . . . . enough to fill and frost a 15 cm (6 inch) layer cake or generously top a loaf cake or frost 12 cupcakes

Prep time . . . . . 5–10 minutes

For the Buttercream

150 g (5½ oz) . . . . unsalted butter, softened
300g (10½ oz) . . . icing sugar
splash . . . . milk (optional; if needed)

Optional Flavourings

1 tablespoon . . . . vanilla paste or extract
1 quantity . . . . . . Cheat's Caramel Sauce (see page 20)
1 quantity . . . . . . Roasted Fruit Compote (see page 21), adding an extra 50 g (1¾ oz) icing sugar to the buttercream

1. Add your butter to a mixing bowl and beat until lighter in colour.
2. Sift in the icing sugar in 3 parts, beating well between each addition to incorporate.
3. Beat for 3–5 minutes until super-light and fluffy, then add in any flavouring, if using. If it is looking a little dry, add a splash of milk to loosen so it's easy to spread or pipe.

BREAD DOUGH

Makes . . . . 1 boule or 8 dinner rolls

Prep time . . . . . 20 minutes, plus 20 minutes resting time

Proving time . . . 40-60 minutes

• Rolls

Proving time . . . 20-30 minutes

Bake time . . . . . 15-20 minutes

• Boule

Proving time . . . 30-40 minutes

Bake time . . . . . 35-45 minutes

For the Dough

250 g (9 oz) . . . . . strong white flour
1 teaspoon. . . . . . fast-action dried yeast
1 teaspoon. . . . . . granulated sugar
½ teaspoon . . . . . salt
170g (6 oz). . . . . . warm water
30 g (1 oz) . . . . . . unsalted butter, melted and cooled, or olive/vegetable oil

This easy bread dough is an almost no-knead situation as the dough is quite wet, so it needs to be 'folded' instead.

1. In a medium bowl, combine the flour, yeast, sugar and salt. Pour in the water and mix to get a sticky, shaggy dough.
2. Pour the melted, cooled butter (or oil) over the dough and squish it in by hand until you get a smooth dough that you can form into a ball.
3. Cover with a clean tea towel and leave to rest for 20 minutes.
4. Uncover the dough. Now we're going to do some stretch-and-folds! Imagine your dough has a north, east, south and west edge. Grab the north edge of the dough and pull it up and over to the south edge of the bowl. Repeat with the other opposite edges of the dough so you've folded all the edges over - this is one set of stretch-and-folds. Repeat this once more so you've done 2 sets.
5. Cover the dough with the tea towel and leave somewhere warm until doubled in size, around 40-60 minutes.

To make a boule:

1. Punch down the dough, then form into a smooth ball. Remove the crisper plate, then line the base of your air fryer with baking paper and brush with a bit of oil. Place the boule in the air fryer drawer, then cover with a tea towel and leave somewhere warm to rise until almost doubled in volume (30-40 minutes).
2. Using a sharp knife, slash the top of the boule in a cross shape, then air fry at 180°C (350°F) for 30-35 minutes until browned on top. Flip it over and air fry for 5-10 minutes to brown the base.
3. Remove to a wire rack to cool completely before slicing.

To make dinner rolls:

1. Punch down the dough, cut into 8 equal pieces then roll each into a ball.
2. Make sure the crisper plate is in the air fryer drawer. Line the base of your air fryer with baking paper and brush with a bit of oil.
3. Place the dough balls in the air fryer then cover with a tea towel and leave somewhere warm to rise until almost doubled in volume (15-25 minutes).
4. Air fry at 180°C (350°F) for 20-30 minutes until golden on top and dry on the bottom.

ROUGH PUFF PASTRY

Makes . . . . about 600 g (1 lb 5 oz)

Prep time . . . . . 30 minutes, plus 1 hour 20 minutes chilling

For the Pastry

250 g (9 oz) . . . . . plain flour, plus extra for dusting

½ teaspoon . . . . . fine salt

225 g (8 oz) . . . . . cold unsalted butter, cut into 1 cm (½ inch) cubes

120 g (4 oz) . . . . . iced water

1 teaspoon. . . . . . lemon juice

Making a proper puff pastry requires more precision and patience than either of us has time for! When you're wanting that same buttery, flaky crust but with half the stress, turn to rough puff pastry instead. You can use this pastry for recipes such as our Cheese & Olive Twists, Flaky Speculoos Apple Pies and Veggie Sausage & Chutney Rolls (see pages 176, 185 and 164).

1. Mix the flour and salt in a medium bowl. Add the butter cubes and toss to coat. Place the bowl in the freezer for 10 minutes to chill everything down.
2. Once chilled, take the bowl out of the freezer and make a well in the centre. Combine the iced water and lemon juice in a jug. Pour in a few tablespoons of the lemony water and work it into the flour with your fingertips, pinching the butter cubes to flatten them slightly; you are not rubbing the butter in here, and lumps of it should still be visible.
3. Drizzle in the remaining water a bit at a time, mixing it in until the dough holds together when squeezed. Knead in the bowl gently to bring it all together into a ball.
4. Tip out onto a piece of clingfilm, pat out into a block about 17 x 12 cm (6½ x 4½ inches), then wrap in the clingfilm and refrigerate for 30 minutes.
5. Roll the pastry out into a rectangle, about 3 times as long as it is wide, dusting with flour as needed to prevent it sticking, then fold into thirds, like a business letter. This is one 'turn'. Rotate the block 90 degrees so that a folded side is now facing you and repeat this roll and fold once more so you've completed 2 'turns'.
6. Refrigerate the pastry for 20 minutes to help firm up the butter again.
7. Complete 2 more 'turns' of the dough, wrap tightly in clingfilm and refrigerate for at least 20 minutes (or up to 3 days), until needed.

SHORTCRUST PASTRY

Makes	300 g (10½ oz) or enough to line a 18 or 20 cm (7 or 8 inch) tart tin or 6 small pastry tins
Prep time	10 minutes

For the Shortcrust Pastry

200 g (7 oz)	plain flour
100 g (3½ oz)	cold butter, cubed
2 teaspoons	caster sugar (for sweet pastry only)
2–3 tablespoons	cold milk or water

A super-simple and versatile pastry used in loads of our recipes, from Jam Tart Bars and Lemon Tarts (see pages 92 and 96) to quiches (see pages 168–9). It bakes really well in the air fryer, but to avoid soggy bottoms make sure you use your crisper plate. You might need to flip any blind-baked shells over to cook through, so use silicone tongs to be as delicate as you can.

1. Grab a mixing bowl and add your flour and butter. Crumble the butter with your fingertips, pressing firmly to squish it with the flour. Mix more flour with the butter and keep rubbing until the mixture looks like fine breadcrumbs. Stir through the sugar, if making sweet pastry.
2. Add the milk or water, 1 tablespoon at a time, using a metal spoon or knife to bring the dough together.
3. Lightly use your hands to shape into a ball and cover in clingfilm or pop in an airtight container until ready to use. (You don't need to chill it yet or it'll be hard to roll!)

CHOUX PASTRY

Makes . . . . enough for 12–15 profiteroles, 6–8 large éclairs or 12 mini éclairs (see Tip below)

Prep time . . . . . 15 minutes, plus cooling

Bake time . . . . . 22 minutes

Equipment

piping bag, parchment or silicone liner

For the Choux Pastry

125 g (4 oz) . . . . . water
50 g (1¾ oz) . . . . . unsalted butter
70 g (2½ oz) . . . . . plain flour
2 . . . . medium eggs, well beaten

TIPS

- For a cheat's pastry cream, add 1 teaspoon each of custard powder and vanilla paste to 100 ml (3½ fl oz) double cream and whisk until thick.
- If making mini éclairs, bake for 10 minutes, reduce the heat as in the main recipe, then bake them for another 10 minutes.

The air fryer is ideal for choux pastry, so if you've had trouble in your oven, give these a go! Fill with vanilla cream and then dip in some melted chocolate for a classic and easy dessert. You will need this recipe for our Pistachio Profiteroles, Éclair Ring Cake and Raspberry Cheesecake Eclairs (see pages 100, 116 and 120).

1. Add the water and butter to a small saucepan and place over a low heat until the butter is melted. Increase the heat and bring up to a boil, then immediately add the flour and beat well with a wooden spoon.
2. Let cook out for a few minutes over the heat until it sticks to itself and is smooth. Remove from the pan and pop into a large mixing bowl to cool. Spread the mixture out up the sides to speed up the cooling.
3. When completely cool, add the egg a small amount at a time, beating really well between each addition (you may find this easier with an electric hand whisk). Add enough egg to make a dropping consistency: when you lift your spoon or whisk up, it should easily drop off back into the bowl.
4. Add whichever nozzle you'd like to your piping bag and then fill with your choux pastry. Line the base of your air fryer with a parchment or silicone liner.
5. Pipe the mixture in your preferred shape - little dollops for profiteroles and buns and lines for éclairs. Leave a 4 cm (1½ inch) gap between each as they will grow! Use scissors to cut the pastry off the nozzle and use a little dab of water to push down any points.
6. Air fry at 180°C (350°F) for 17 minutes then reduce the temperature down to 160°C (325°F) and continue to bake for 5 minutes until puffed up and golden brown.
7. Remove straight away from the air fryer, using silicone tongs, then poke a hole in the bottom of each with a knife before leaving to cool completely on a wire rack.
8. Fill with a flavoured whipped cream and some of our Roasted Fruit Compotes (see page 21) and pile your creations up on a platter for a speedy showstopper.

CHEAT'S CARAMEL SAUCE

Makes . . . . 250 ml (9 fl oz)

Prep time . . . . . 5 minutes

Bake time . . . . . 15–20 minutes

Equipment

baking dish or cake tin (not loose-bottomed) that fits in your air fryer

For the Sauce

100 g (3½ oz) . . . . soft light brown sugar

50 g (1¾ oz) . . . . . unsalted butter, cut into a few cubes

120 ml (4 fl oz) . . . double cream

¼ teaspoon . . . . . fine salt

The perfect thing for drizzling over ice cream or cake, this caramel sauce comes together easily in the air fryer. We're calling this a cheat's version as it relies on the caramelly richness of brown sugar to bring depth of flavour without actually caramelizing the sugar. This sauce is delicious served with our Chocolate Fondants, Pavlova or Roasted Banana Boats (see pages 60, 66 and 77).

1. Place the sugar in the dish or tin, and place the butter pieces on top of the sugar.
2. Air fry at 180°C (350°F) for 3–5 minutes, until the butter has melted, then stir in the cream. Air fry for a further 10–15 minutes, stirring halfway through, until bubbling and slightly thickened.
3. Carefully remove from the air fryer and stir in the salt. Serve warm or allow to cool, then store in a clean jar in the refrigerator for up to 1 week.

TIP

- For an easy toffee sauce, just replace the light brown sugar with dark brown sugar. Perfect for sticky toffee pud!

ROASTED FRUIT COMPOTES

Makes	200–300 ml (⅓–½ pint)
Prep time	5 minutes
Bake time	15–20 minutes

Equipment

small ceramic baking dish or cake tin

Berry or Rhubarb

400 g (14 oz)	berries: strawberries, blueberries, blackberries or raspberries, or 400 g (14 oz) rhubarb, cut into 2–3 cm (¾–1¼ inch) pieces
75–100 g (2¾–3½ oz)	caster sugar

Stone Fruit

300 g (10½ oz)	pitted weight: plums, peaches or nectarines
60–80 g (2¼–3 oz)	caster sugar

Apples or Pears

4	apples or pears, peeled and cored
75–100 g (2½–3½ oz)	honey or maple syrup
1 teaspoon	ground cinnamon (optional)

Roasting fruit gives it such a rich flavour, and these compotes can be used for all manner of bakes. We've got them topping our Simple Scones (see page 102) and Burnt Basque Cheesecake (see page 152) but you can serve it over ice cream, or slather it straight on to toast. We find using a single fruit gives the best hit of flavour, but if you like a mix, we're not going to stop you...

Berry or Rhubarb:

If using strawberries, remove the hulls and then slice in half. Add the fruit to a bowl and toss in the sugar. Pour into the baking dish or cake tin, then air fry at 160°C (325°F) for 15–20 minutes, stirring every 5 minutes. You can continue to cook down for a softer compote, or blend and strain through a sieve to a smooth purée.

Stone Fruit:

Cut the fruit into wedges or chunks, add to a bowl, toss with the sugar then follow the baking instructions left.

Apples or Pears:

Chop your apples or pears into 2 cm (¾ inch) cubes. Add to a bowl, drizzle over the honey or maple syrup then follow the instructions left. Bramley apples will cook down faster and be done nearer the 15-minute mark.

2

BREAKFAST BITES

Everyone knows that starting your morning with a quick, filling meal sets you up for success in the day ahead. It can be hard to find inspiration, so let the air fryer give you a helping hand with satisfying recipes that are a snap to make.

(ALMOST) INSTANT BAGELS

Makes 2

Prep time . . . . . 10 minutes, plus 30 minutes resting

Bake time . . . . . 17–20 minutes

Equipment

baking paper

For the Bagels

100 g (3½ oz). . . . self-raising flour
¼ teaspoon . . . . . fine salt
½ teaspoon . . . . . fast-action dried yeast
100 g (3½ oz). . . . 0% fat Greek yogurt
1 tablespoon . . . . mixed seeds

Traditionally, bagels are boiled before baking to give them a shiny crust and chewy texture. This recipe skips the boiling step (which technically means they aren't true 'bagels'), instead using Greek yogurt in the dough to give them that toothsome texture. You'll get 2 bagels out of this recipe, so you can have the first freshly baked and the second the next day. We like to halve the day-old bagel and toast it, cut sides up, in the air fryer at 200°C (400°F) for 1–2 minutes until warmed through.

1. Mix the flour, salt and yeast in a medium bowl. Add the yogurt and stir together, then knead in the bowl until you get a smooth, firm dough. Add a splash of water (2–3 teaspoons) if it seems a bit dry. Cover and leave to rest for 30 minutes.
2. Divide the dough in half. Roll each half into a ball and poke a hole in the middle of each. Stretch out to form a ring shape - you want the hole in the centre to be about 5 cm (2 inches) across (or the hole may disappear on baking!).
3. Line the base of your air fryer with baking paper. Place the bagels in the air fryer, brush with water, then sprinkle with the mixed seeds.
4. Air fry at 160°C (325°F) for 15 minutes, then flip and bake for another 2–4 minutes until golden underneath. Allow to cool before serving. Store at room temperature in a sealed container for up to 2 days. It's best to reheat them by slicing in half and air frying at 180°C (350°F) for 1–2 minutes (or reheat in a toaster).

MIXED SEED GRANOLA

Makes . . . . about 450 g (1 lb) or 8 portions

Prep time . . . . . 5 minutes

Bake time . . . . . 25–30 minutes

Equipment

parchment or silicone liner

For the Granola

50 g (1¾ oz) . . . . . melted butter or coconut/vegetable oil

75 g (2½ oz) . . . . . honey or maple syrup

250 g (9 oz) . . . . . jumbo rolled oats

100 g (3½ oz) . . . . mixed seeds: pumpkin, sesame, sunflower

pinch. . . . . fine salt

50 g (1¾ oz) . . . . . mixed nuts and/or crystallized ginger, chopped (optional)

Making a week's worth of granola on a Sunday allows you to change up your flavours every week! Just keep the oats, honey and butter or oil the same and then let your imagination run wild. This is great for breakfast with yogurt, or even use it to top the Fruited Bran Muffins on page 32 for an extra crunch on them.

1. Add your melted butter or oil, sweetener of choice, oats and seeds to a large bowl. Stir well to combine, adding a pinch of salt to taste. If using the nuts or crystallized ginger, add them too.
2. Tip into your silicone or parchment liner and flatten with the back of a spoon. Remove the crisper plate from your air fryer and air fry at 150°C (300°F) for 15 minutes. Use a spatula to break up the granola and toss it gently. Air fry for another 10–15 minutes, until deep golden brown.
3. Pull the air fryer basket out and allow the granola to cool in there completely before gently breaking up and storing in an airtight container for up to 2 months.

ALMOND CROISSANT TOAST

Serves. 2

Prep time . . . . . 5 minutes

Bake time . . . . . 7–12 minutes

Equipment

piping bag (optional)

For the Croissant Toast

20 g (¾ oz). . . . . . salted butter, softened

40 g (1½ oz) . . . . . soft light brown, granulated or caster sugar

½ tablespoon . . . plain flour

1 . . . . large egg white

⅛ teaspoon. . . . . almond extract

50 g (1¾ oz) . . . . . ground almonds

2 slices . . . . day-old brioche or 2 day-old croissants

1 tablespoon . . . . apricot jam

2 tablespoons . . . flaked almonds

pinch. . . . . icing sugar (optional)

This recipe is based on a French breakfast pastry known as bostock that we both love - it involves soaking stale brioche slices in syrup, then spreading them with jam and frangipane before baking. The result is a bready pastry that reminds us of almond croissants. Here we've made a simplified version of it, skipping the syrup soaking as we find it plenty sweet already. If you have stale croissants rather than brioche, you can do as the bakeries do and use the jam and frangipane combo to make a homemade almond croissant instead.

1. In a medium bowl, mix the butter and sugar until smooth. Stir in the flour, egg white and almond extract. Finally, mix in the ground almonds.
2. If using brioche, spread each slice with ½ tablespoon of apricot jam then thickly spread (or pipe) the almond mixture on top. Sprinkle with the flaked almonds.
3. If using croissants, cut them in half. Sandwich the jam and three quarters of the almond mixture between the 2 halves of each croissant. Spread the remaining almond mixture on top of the croissants and sprinkle with the flaked almonds.
4. Air fry the brioche or croissants at 160°C (325°F) for 7–12 minutes. For the brioche, the topping should be golden around the edges and feel set to the touch. For the croissants, the topping should be golden and the inside slightly gooey.
5. Allow to cool for a few minutes before dusting with icing sugar, if you like, and digging in.

CRUMPET LOAF

Makes . . . . 1 loaf

Prep time . . . . . 10 minutes, plus 1 hour 10 minutes resting

Bake time . . . . . 30–40 minutes

Equipment

450 g (1 lb) metal loaf tin, buttered

For the Crumpet Loaf

200 g (7 oz) . . . . . strong white flour
1½ teaspoons . . . fast-action dried yeast
1 teaspoon. . . . . . baking powder
¼ teaspoon . . . . . fine salt
180 g (6½ oz) . . . . warm water
1 tablespoon . . . . vegetable oil

As bread loaves go, this is a pretty easy one to rustle up. Yes, it does require some rising time but the dough is quick to mix as it's very wet, and it only needs to be mixed briefly by hand instead of being kneaded. The baking powder combined with the wetness of the dough makes for a spongey-textured loaf, akin to a crumpet, hence the name!

1. In a medium bowl, combine the flour, yeast, baking powder and salt, mixing well. Pour in the water and mix to get a soft, scraggly dough. Beat well using your hand in the shape of a paddle for 1–2 minutes, taking breaks as needed, then scrape down the sides of the bowl and cover with a clean tea towel.
2. Leave somewhere warm for 20–30 minutes to rest. It will have almost doubled in volume and look bubbly.
3. Drizzle the oil over the dough and use your fingertips to pull the edges of the dough away from the sides of the bowl, folding them in towards the centre. Lift the dough out of the bowl and into the buttered loaf tin. Cover with the tea towel and leave until the dough has risen up to the rim of the tin, 30–40 minutes.
4. Air fry at 180°C (350°F) for 30–40 minutes until golden all over. Tip out of the tin on to a wire rack and leave to cool completely before slicing up.

FRUITED BRAN MUFFINS

Makes 6

Prep time . . . . . 10 minutes, plus 20–30 minutes soaking

Bake time . . . . . 23–28 minutes

Equipment

6 large silicone muffin cases

For the Bran Muffins

75 g (2½ oz) . . . . . bran flakes
200 ml (7 fl oz). . . milk
125 g (4½ oz) . . . . dried fruit (we like a mix of apple, blueberries, cherries and cranberries)
100 g (3½ oz). . . . boiling water
100 g (3½ oz). . . . natural or Greek yogurt
1 . . . . large egg
50 g (1¾ oz) . . . . . honey
1 tablespoon . . . . black treacle
100 g (3½ oz). . . . wholemeal flour
1 teaspoon. . . . . . baking powder
½ teaspoon . . . . . bicarbonate of soda
pinch. . . . . fine salt

These are such a great start to the day, and are packed full of fibre. It's worth getting a nice variety of dried fruits to keep them super soft. They freeze well too, so it's good to make a few batches for emergency breakfasts on the go – just let them defrost overnight at room temperature.

1. Add your bran flakes to a small bowl and cover with the milk. Add the dried fruit to another bowl and cover with the boiling water. Leave both to soak for 20–30 minutes or until the bran is soft and the fruit plump.
2. Add the yogurt, egg, honey and treacle to a mixing bowl and whisk well to combine. Pour in the softened bran flakes and milk and whisk again.
3. Fold in the flour, baking powder, bicarbonate of soda and salt, then strain your fruit and add this to the batter, stirring until evenly mixed.
4. Divide between the 6 muffin cases – you can fill them near to the top as they don't rise a huge amount!
5. Air fry at 160°C (325°F) for 23–28 minutes until risen, golden brown and a cocktail stick inserted into the middle comes out with just a few crumbs on. Leave to cool for a few minutes before removing from the cases.

MAPLE BAKED FRENCH TOAST

Serves. 2

Prep time . . . . . 20 minutes

Bake time . . . . . 15–20 minutes

Equipment

parchment or silicone liner (one with a base and sides)

For the French Toast

1 . . . . large egg
1 . . . . teaspoon ground cinnamon
1 . . . . teaspoon vanilla paste
pinch. . . . . salt
100 ml (3½ fl oz). . milk
3 tablespoons . . . maple syrup
2. . . . . very thick slices soft white bread, about 100 g (3½ oz) each
1 tablespoon . . . . soft light brown sugar
10 g (¼ oz) . . . . . . salted butter, cut into little cubes

To serve

Salted butter
Greek yogurt
Fresh berries

Here we take thick, fluffy slices of bread and soak them in a simple cinnamon-y custard. This is the way we'd usually start off a recipe for traditional French toast, which is pan fried and served with maple syrup poured on top. However, for this one we've air fried that custardy bread on a layer of butter, brown sugar and maple syrup which caramelizes on the toast as it cooks. The result is a soft-centred slice, with a crunchy, crispy crust. Serve it up with salty butter and fruit for a heavenly brunch experience.

1. Mix the egg, cinnamon, vanilla and salt in a wide, shallow dish. Pour in the milk and 1 tablespoon of the maple syrup then whisk to combine fully.
2. Add the bread slices and turn to coat fully in the milk mixture. Let them sit for 10 minutes to absorb the remaining liquid, flipping them over halfway through to get them evenly soaked.
3. Add the liner to your air fryer. Sprinkle the sugar over the base and drizzle with 1 tablespoon of the maple syrup. Dot with the butter cubes, trying to space them out evenly.
4. Place the soaked bread slices on top of the butter and air fry at 180°C (350°F) for 10–15 minutes, flipping them over halfway, until starting to caramelize.
5. Pour ½ tablespoon of the remaining maple syrup over each bread slice and return to the air fryer for a final 5 minutes to get crispy.
6. Remove from the air fryer to plates and serve with a pat of salted butter on top, and yogurt and berries on the side.

TIPS

- It's best to buy an unsliced white bread loaf from the bakery section of the supermarket and use that to get your thick slices of bread. We like to use a 400 g (14 oz) loaf (which would give you 4 thick slices), removing the ends of the loaf before slicing it up.
- You can easily double the recipe, but you'll likely need to air fry it in batches.

PICKLED JALAPEÑO, CORN & HALLOUMI MUFFINS

Makes 9

Prep time . . . . . 10 minutes

Bake time . . . . . 15–18 minutes

Equipment

9 large (175 ml/6 fl oz) silicone or paper muffin cases (see page 10)

For the Muffins

½ small jar . . . . . . pickled green jalapeños, about 50 g (1¾ oz) drained weight (save the pickling liquor, see below), roughly chopped

1 small can . . . . . . sweetcorn (150 g/5½ oz drained weight)

1 x 225 g (8 oz) . . . block halloumi

150 g (5½ oz) . . . . self-raising flour

½ teaspoon . . . . . baking powder

½ teaspoon . . . . . bicarbonate of soda

½ teaspoon . . . . . fine salt

100 ml (3½ fl oz). . jalapeño pickling liquor from the jar

50 ml (2 fl oz) . . . . milk

1 . . . . large egg

50 ml (2 fl oz) . . . . vegetable oil

After taco night you might have half a jar of these delicious pickled jalapeños hanging around in the refrigerator, or if you're a chilli lover, buy a jar especially! Make a batch at the beginning of the week and take a couple for brekkie on the go. They are an ideal picnic bite too.

1. Add the chopped jalapeños to a large bowl with your drained sweetcorn.
2. Grate the halloumi and dab with kitchen paper to remove any excess liquid. Pop into the bowl with the jalapeños and sweetcorn. Add the flour, baking powder, bicarbonate of soda and salt and toss well to coat.
3. Add the reserved, measured pickling liquor to a jug then add the milk – don't worry if it curdles, it makes fluffy muffins!
4. Add the egg and oil and whisk until blended before pouring into the dry ingredients, mixing lightly until only just combined.
5. Place the cupcake cases in the air fryer and divide the batter evenly between them – you can fill them right to the top. Air fry at 160°C (325°F) for 15–18 minutes or until slightly risen and golden brown.

TIP

- Use the whole jar of jalapeños if you like it spicy!

CARROT CAKE BAKED OATS

Serves. 2

Prep time . . . . . 20 minutes

Bake time . . . . . 15 minutes

Equipment

15 cm (6 inch) round cake tin or ceramic/enamel baking dish, greased

For the Oats

50 g (1¾ oz) . . . . . raisins
50 g (2 oz) . . . . . . boiling water
1 . . . . medium carrot, grated
150 g (5½ oz) . . . . porridge oats
1 tablespoon . . . . chia seeds
1–2 teaspoons . . . ground cinnamon
50 ml (2 fl oz) . . . . maple syrup, honey or agave
2 . . . . large eggs, lightly beaten, or 1 large banana, mashed
100 g (3½ oz) . . . . walnuts or pecans

To serve

Greek or oat yogurt

On a chilly morning, there's nothing better than a warming bowl for breakfast, and these are a super-hearty and healthy way to start your day! You can double the recipe easily and make 4 ramekins for the week if you'd prefer. Keep the baking time the same, as they'll be slightly deeper.

1. Add the raisins to a small bowl, pour over the boiling water and leave to soak for 15 minutes.
2. Put the grated carrot, oats, chia seeds, cinnamon, maple syrup or honey/agave and egg or banana into a bowl. Stir well, then pour in the raisins and their soaking liquid. Add the nuts and mix to combine.
3. Spoon the mixture into the prepared tin or dish and air fry at 160°C (325°F) for 15 minutes, until set and golden brown.
4. Serve straight away for a warm breakfast with a dollop of yogurt, or this keeps really well in the refrigerator over night for meal prep: reheat in the air fryer at 160°C (325°F) for 5 minutes.

STOUT SODA BREAD

Makes . . . . 1 loaf

Prep time . . . . . 10 minutes

Bake time . . . . . 35 minutes

Equipment

parchment or silicone liner

For the Soda Bread

150 ml (¼ pint) . . . milk
1 teaspoon . . . . . lemon juice
230 g (8¼ oz) . . . . wholemeal flour
220 g (8 oz) . . . . . plain flour
8 g (¼ oz) . . . . bicarbonate of soda
½ teaspoon . . . . . fine salt
75 g (2½ oz) . . . . . porridge oats
25 g (1 oz) . . . . cold salted butter, cubed
1 teaspoon . . . . . . honey
1 teaspoon . . . . . . black treacle or molasses
½ x 400 ml (14 fl oz) . . . . . . can stout (use a can rather than a bottle for extra bubbles)

To serve

Butter, jam or fruit compote

Bubbly bicarbonate of soda and the world-famous Irish stout work together beautifully here to provide the rise in this delicious loaf. Perfect on the day it's made, it also makes amazing toast to take you through the week.

1. Start by making your buttermilk by mixing the milk with the lemon juice in a jug and letting it sit for 5 minutes.
2. Add your dry ingredients to a large mixing bowl and whisk together. Rub in the cold butter until the mixture looks like breadcrumbs. (It will be harder to do than pastry but should be an even texture.) Make a well in the centre.
3. Add your honey, black treacle or molasses and stout to the buttermilk mixture and stir well. Slowly add the wet to the dry ingredients and mix thoroughly until a soft, sticky dough forms.
4. Place the liner in your air fryer and tip the dough out on to the work surface. Knead slightly to bring it together, then shape into a gentle round, or boule, and place on the liner. Use scissors or a knife to make a cross in the top.
5. Air fry at 190°C (375°F) for 20 minutes before carefully turning over and baking upside down for a further 10 minutes. Turn the bread back over and air fry for a final 5 minutes (it's cooked through when it sounds hollow when tapped on the bottom). Carefully remove the loaf from the air fryer and leave to cool for at least an hour on a wire rack.

3

CLASSIC FAVOURITES

Classics are classic for a reason – we all know and love them! You may have made these recipes with your gran growing up, but we're here to give them an air fryer shake up, so they are easier to make than you thought possible.

SHINY TOP BROWNIES

Makes 9

Prep time . . . . . 15 minutes

Bake time . . . . . 20–25 minutes

Equipment

15 or 18 cm (6 or 7 inch) square cake tin, base and sides lined with a sling of baking paper, secured with metal binder clips (see page 10)

For the Brownies

100 g (3½ oz) . . . . plain dark chocolate, minimum 70% cocoa solids, broken into pieces
100 g (3½ oz) . . . . unsalted butter
2 . . . . large eggs
200 g (7 oz) . . . . . caster sugar
¼ teaspoon . . . . . fine salt
1 teaspoon. . . . . . vanilla extract
60 g (2¼ oz) . . . . . plain flour

Brownies are one of our go-to desserts, because you can make them quickly and they're always a crowd pleaser! We like to err on the side of slightly underbaked as they firm up nicely once cooled, giving them a really fudgy texture. By briefly whisking the sugar with the eggs, some of the sugar gets dissolved, which gives the brownies their shiny tops. Don't go overboard with the whisking, though, as that will make them moussey, rather than fudgy.

1. Melt the chocolate and butter together in a heatproof bowl set over a pan of simmering water. Alternatively, melt together in the microwave in a heatproof, microwave-safe bowl in 45-second bursts, until smooth.
2. Place the eggs and sugar in a medium bowl and whisk together for 2–3 minutes until slightly paler and aerated (we like to use an electric whisk for this as it really helps dissolve the sugar, but you can just whisk by hand using a balloon whisk).
3. Pour the melted chocolate and butter mixture into the whisked eggs and stir together until fully mixed. Add the salt and vanilla and stir these in well. Add the flour and fold together until combined, then pour into the lined tin.
4. Air fry at 160°C (325°F) for 20–25 minutes – they're done when the middle is still a bit gooey (a toothpick inserted into the centre will come out with sticky crumbs) and the edges are set; it'll set fully once cooled so it's best to not overbake these!
5. Leave to cool at room temperature, then refrigerate for around an hour to let them fully set before slicing into 9 squares.

CAPPUCCINO & CARAMELIZED WALNUT CAKE

Serves 4–6

Prep time . . . . . 25 minutes

Bake time . . . . . 35–45 minutes

Equipment

18 cm (7 inch) deep, round cake tin, greased and lined

For the Cake

2 . . . . large eggs
150 g (5½ oz) . . . . soft light brown sugar
100 g (3½ oz) . . . . walnut halves or pieces
110 g (3¾ oz) . . . . unsalted butter, softened
1 tablespoon . . . . instant coffee granules
2 tablespoons . . . hot water
110 g (3¾ oz) . . . . self-raising flour
1 teaspoon. . . . . . baking powder
pinch. . . . . salt

For the Frosting

1 tablespoon . . . . instant coffee granules
1 tablespoon . . . . hot water
75 g (2½ oz) . . . . . unsalted butter, softened
150 g (5½ oz) . . . . icing sugar
pinch. . . . . salt
1 teaspoon. . . . . . unsweetened cocoa powder, to finish

To give the classic coffee walnut cake a bit of a jazzy spin, we caramelize the walnuts first in a mixture of egg white and light brown sugar, which gives a crispy coating. The caramelized walnuts are then folded into the batter, with some also used to decorate. We give the cake a dusting of cocoa powder as well, in a nod to cocoa-dusted cappuccinos.

1. Separate one of the eggs, setting aside the yolk and adding the white to a medium bowl with 50 g (1¾ oz) of the sugar. Mix together, then stir in the walnuts. Use a fork to remove the walnuts from the egg white mixture, letting excess drip off, and place on a piece of baking paper cut to the size of your air fryer crisper plate.
2. Air fry at 180°C (350°F) for 6–8 minutes, stirring halfway, until caramelized and fragrant. Set aside to cool, then finely chop half the walnuts (use the smaller pieces for this, saving any bigger ones for decoration).
3. In a medium bowl, cream together the butter and remaining sugar until smooth. In a cup, mix the instant coffee and hot water until dissolved. Add to the butter mixture and stir together. Beat in the whole egg, reserved egg yolk and any of the leftover egg white and brown sugar mixture. The mixture may look curdled but this is fine!
4. Add the flour, baking powder and salt. Stir until no floury patches remain; don't overmix. Fold in the chopped caramelized walnuts, then scrape the batter into the prepared cake tin and spread out in an even layer.
5. Air fry at 160°C (325°F) for 25 minutes, then turn the temperature down to 150°C (300°F) and air fry for another 10–15 minutes, until a toothpick inserted into the centre comes out clean. Let the cake rest in the tin for 10 minutes, then turn out on to a wire rack and leave to cool completely.
6. For the frosting, combine the instant coffee and hot water in a small bowl, stirring to dissolve, and set aside to cool to room temperature. Cream together the softened butter and icing sugar until smooth, then mix in the cooled coffee and the salt.
7. Ice the cooled cake with the coffee frosting and decorate with the remaining caramelized walnuts and a dusting of cocoa powder.

BREAD & BUTTER PUDDING

Serves 2

Prep time . . . . . 15 minutes

Bake time . . . . . 30–35 minutes

Equipment

19 cm (7½ inch) ceramic baking dish, 6 cm (2½ inches) high, generously buttered

For the Pudding

3–4 thick slices . . stale bread, brioche, hot cross buns or panettone (the end of a loaf is perfect for this!)

40 g (1½ oz) . . . . . unsalted butter, softened

30 g (1 oz) . . . . . . mixed dried fruit or raisins

150 ml (¼ pint) . . . milk

150 ml (¼ pint) . . . double cream, plus extra to serve

2 tablespoons . . . caster sugar

2 . . . . medium eggs

1 . . . . orange or lemon, finely zested

2 tablespoons . . . demerara sugar

We've gone with a classic flavour in our base recipe here, but seasonal variations take this up a notch – hot cross buns and panettone both make for delicious desserts. Sub the raisins for chocolate chips if you like, or add mixed peel if you like things citrusy!

1. Start by buttering your bread really thickly and then cutting each slice into 4 (either triangles or squares). Add them to your buttered baking dish, buttered side up, scattering in the mixed fruit between each piece. Make sure the fruit isn't directly on top or it'll burn!
2. Measure the milk and cream into a jug and add the caster sugar, eggs and citrus zest. Whisk well, then pour over your buttered bread and leave to soak for 10 minutes.
3. Sprinkle over your demerara sugar, cover the dish in foil and air fry at 180°C (350°F) for 20 minutes before removing the foil and baking for another 10–15 minutes until puffed up, golden brown and crispy on top. Either divide between 2 bowls or dive straight into the dish with extra cold cream!

BANANA BREAD

Makes . . . . 1 loaf cake

Prep time . . . . . 5 minutes

Bake time . . . . . 45–50 minutes

Equipment

450 g (1 lb) loaf tin, greased and lined; foil

For the Banana Bread

3 . . . . medium very ripe/brown bananas, about 225 g (8 oz)

75 g (2½ oz) . . . . . soft light brown sugar

100 g (3½ oz) . . . . unsalted butter, melted, or 125 ml (3½ fl oz) vegetable oil

150 g (5½ oz) . . . . self-raising flour

¼ teaspoon . . . . . baking powder

¼ teaspoon . . . . . bicarbonate of soda

1 teaspoon. . . . . . ground cinnamon or 75 g (2½ oz) chocolate chips (optional)

1 tablespoon . . . . demerara sugar (optional)

Forgotten bananas find a new life in this classic recipe, but if your bananas aren't ripe or brown enough, pop them in your air fryer in their skins for 10 minutes at 180°C (350°F). Leave to cool for 5 minutes before using.

1. Start by mashing the bananas with a fork in a mixing bowl. Add in the light brown sugar and melted butter or oil and whisk with the fork to combine.
2. Add in the flour, baking powder and bicarbonate of soda and fold in. Mix in the cinnamon or chocolate chips, if using, then pour the mixture into the prepared loaf tin.
3. Sprinkle over the demerara sugar if you like a little crunchy topping, and air fry at 160°C (325°F) for 20 minutes. Cover with foil and air fry for a further 25–30 minutes or until a skewer inserted into the centre comes out with just a few crumbs on. Leave to cool in the tin for an hour before slicing and serving.

TIP

- If you have any left after 3–4 days, this banana bread is wonderful air fried in slices at 200°C (400°F) for 5 minutes and slathered in butter!

CHOCOLATE FUDGE CAKE

Serves 8–10

Prep time . . . . . 20 minutes

Bake time . . . . . 55 minutes

Equipment

18 cm (7 inch) round cake tin or silicone liner, greased and lined, foil

For the Cake

175 g (6 oz) . . . . . . butter, softened, or margarine
175 g (6 oz) . . . . . . any sugar
3 . . . . large eggs
125 g (4½ oz) . . . . self-raising flour
50 g (1¾ oz) . . . . . unsweetened cocoa powder
1 teaspoon . . . . . instant coffee granules
¼ teaspoon . . . . . fine salt
50 g (1¾ oz) . . . . . soured cream or crème fraîche
splash . . . . milk (optional)

For the Frosting

50 g (1¾ oz) . . . . . unsalted butter
125 g (4½ oz) . . . . plain dark chocolate, 70% cocoa solids, chopped
100 g (3½ oz) . . . . soured cream or crème fraîche
250 g (9 oz) . . . . . icing sugar

Rich, decadent and chocolatey: all the best things a fudge cake can be! We've made a super-simple frosting to go with it - a great chocolate base with a bit of sharpness from the soured cream helps to cut through the richness of the cake.

1. Add the butter or margarine and the sugar to a mixing bowl and beat well until light and fluffy. Add the eggs then beat again until smooth. Add the flour, cocoa, coffee and salt and fold gently through until evenly combined. Stir through the soured cream or crème fraîche (with a splash of milk if it's a little thick), then pour into the prepared cake tin.
2. Air fry at 160°C (325°F) for 20 minutes, then cover with foil and bake for a further 35 minutes until a toothpick inserted into the centre comes out clean. Leave to cool for 10 minutes in the air fryer before turning out on to a wire rack and leaving to cool completely.
3. Meanwhile, melt the butter and chocolate for the frosting in the microwave in a large heatproof and microwave-safe bowl in 45 second bursts, until smooth. Let cool to room temperature.
4. Add the soured cream or crème fraîche, then sift in the icing sugar a little at a time, beating well after each addition to keep it smooth. You may need to add a splash of hot water if it gets a bit thick.
5. When the cake is cool, cut it carefully in half horizontally to give you 2 cakes. Add half of your frosting to the top of one, then pop the other cake on top. Finish with the remaining frosting, swooping and swirling as you like.

FLAPJACKS

Makes 9

Prep time . . . . . 10 minutes

Bake time . . . . . 15–20 minutes

Equipment

15 or 18 cm (6 or 7 inch) square cake tin, base and sides lined with a sling of baking paper, secured with metal binder clips (see page 10)

For the Flapjacks

75 g (2½ oz) . . . . . unsalted butter
40 g (1½ oz) . . . . . golden syrup
80 g (3 oz) . . . . . . soft light brown sugar
¼ teaspoon . . . . . fine salt
110 g (3¾ oz) . . . . porridge oats
40 g (1½ oz) . . . . . plain flour
100 g (3½ oz). . . . mix-ins, such as nuts, dried fruit, seeds, chocolate chips (optional)

When butter, oats and golden syrup combine, the flavour created is something quite magical – these flapjacks are a fab example! If you're a purist you can keep them plain, but it's effortless to customize them with your favourite mix-ins, too.

1. Place the butter, syrup, sugar and salt in a medium pan over a medium heat, stirring often until the butter has melted and the mixture starts to bubble. Remove from the heat and stir in the oats and flour. Stir in any mix-ins now, if using (apart from chocolate chips).
2. Press the mixture into the prepared tin and air fry at 160°C (325°F) for 15–20 minutes until deep golden on top.
3. Remove from the air fryer and, if using chocolate chips, sprinkle them on now while the flapjacks are warm so that they melt and adhere to the surface.
4. Let the flapjacks cool in the tin for 10 minutes before lifting out on to a wire rack, then leave to cool completely before cutting into 9 squares with a sharp knife.

SHORTBREAD

Serves 8

Prep time . . . . . 10 minutes

Bake time . . . . . 40–45 minutes

Equipment

18 cm (7 inch) loose-bottomed round cake tin, lined

For the Shortbread

150 g (5½ oz) . . . . plain flour
45 g (1½ oz) . . . . . caster sugar, plus extra for sprinkling
pinch. . . . . fine salt
100 g (3½ oz). . . . cold unsalted butter, cubed

A rich, buttery shortbread is nothing short of perfection, especially when homemade. The key is a low and slow bake which helps dry the shortbread out without letting it get too caramelized.

1. Place all the dry ingredients in a medium bowl and mix together using your fingertips. Rub the butter into the dry ingredients until you get a crumbly mixture.
2. Tip into the prepared cake tin and spread out into an even layer before pressing down firmly.
3. Prick with a fork all over, then air fry at 140°C (275°F) for 30 minutes. Score the shortbread into 8 wedges then return to the air fryer for a further 10–15 minutes until dry but still quite pale. It'll feel slightly soft while warm but will crisp up as it cools.
4. Sprinkle with a thin layer of caster sugar, then leave to cool for 10 minutes, before removing from the tin on to a wire rack to cool completely.
5. Break along the score lines and eat! Store leftovers in an airtight container for up to 2 weeks.

CRACKLY LEMON DRIZZLE CAKE

Makes . . . . 1 loaf cake

Prep time . . . . . 10 minutes

Cook time . . . . . 30–35 minutes

Equipment

450 g (1 lb) loaf tin, base and sides lined with a sling of baking paper, secured with metal binder clips (see page 10)

For the Cake

100 g (3½ oz) . . . . granulated or caster sugar
1 . . . . lemon, finely zested
1 . . . . medium egg
75 g (2½ oz) . . . . . full-fat natural yogurt
50 g (1¾ oz) . . . . . vegetable oil
pinch. . . . . fine salt
100 g (3½ oz) . . . . self-raising flour

For the Glaze

60 g (2¼ oz). . . . . granulated sugar
1 . . . . lemon, juiced

A whisk-together batter makes this loaf cake really quick to prep. By rubbing the lemon zest into the sugar, the flavourful lemon oils are drawn out, giving the cake a deep, citrusy flavour. Pouring a combination of granulated sugar and lemon juice over the warm cake, then letting it cool, results in a unique crunchy glaze.

1. In a medium bowl, rub together the sugar and lemon zest until pale yellow and fragrant. Add the egg, yogurt, oil and salt and whisk together until well combined. Add the flour and stir until just combined.
2. Pour the batter into the prepared loaf tin and air fry at 160°C (325°F) for 30–35 minutes, until well browned and a toothpick inserted into the centre of the cake comes out clean.
3. Make the glaze by mixing together the sugar and lemon juice in a small bowl. Poke holes all over the warm cake with a skewer, then spoon the glaze all over. Leave in the tin to cool completely. Once cooled, lift the cake out of the tin, slice and serve.

DORSET APPLE CAKE

Serves. 8–10

Prep time . . . . . 15 minutes

Bake time . . . . . 1 hour 20 minutes to 1 hour 30 minutes

Equipment

20 cm (8 inch) round cake tin, greased and lined, foil

For the Cake

175 g (6 oz). . . . . . butter, softened
175 g (6 oz). . . . . . soft light or dark brown sugar
3. . . . . eggs
175 g (6 oz). . . . . . self-raising flour
2 teaspoons . . . . ground cinnamon
splash . . . . milk or apple juice
3. . . . . large green apples (Bramley or Granny Smith), about 400 g (14 oz) in total
1 tablespoon . . . . demerara sugar

Buttery and moist, with bites of sharp, sweet apple, this cake is an oldie and goodie for a reason. Bramley apples are best, when they're in season, but any green apple will still be delicious all year round.

1. Add the softened butter and brown sugar to a mixing bowl and either beat by hand or use a handheld electric mixer until light and fluffy.
2. Crack in your eggs and beat well before adding in the flour and cinnamon. Fold to mix, then add the splash of milk or apple juice, mix until smooth and pop aside.
3. Peel and core your apples, then slice into wedges.
4. Add half your cake batter to your lined tin and then scatter over half the apple wedges. Add the remaining batter and then the remaining apples, poking them down slightly to nestle them into the cake. Sprinkle the demerara sugar evenly over the top.
5. Air fry at 160°C (325°F) for 35 minutes before covering with foil and air frying for a further 45–55 minutes or until risen and a skewer inserted into the centre comes out clean.

STICKY GINGER CAKE

Makes . . . . 1 loaf cake

Prep time . . . . . 15 minutes

Bake time . . . . . 55 minutes

Equipment

450 g (1 lb) loaf tin, greased and lined, foil

For the Cake

150 g (5½ oz) . . . . fresh root ginger, peeled
100 g (3½ oz). . . . butter or margarine
100 g (3½ oz). . . . black treacle
50 g (1¾ oz) . . . . . light or dark brown soft sugar
50 g (1¾ oz) . . . . . golden syrup
100 ml (3½ fl oz). . milk
2. . . . . large eggs
3 teaspoons . . . . ground ginger
150 g (5½ oz) . . . . self-raising flour
½ teaspoon . . . . . baking powder

For the Icing (optional)

150 g (5½ oz) . . . . icing sugar
1 . . . . lemon, lime or ½ orange, juiced

Zingy, fresh and gets better with age! We've used fresh ginger to maximize the zing, and a bright lemon icing to add some zest. Leave your cake for a day or two before icing, for the squidgiest texture and richest flavour.

1. Start by grating your fresh ginger on the small side of a box grater. You can also run your knife through it afterwards to make sure it's really finely chopped up.
2. Either in a small heatproof and microwave-proof bowl in the microwave or in a small saucepan on the stove, gently melt together the butter or margarine, treacle, sugar and golden syrup.
3. Meanwhile, mix together the milk and eggs in a jug until smooth. Whisk the ground ginger, flour and baking powder together in a large bowl, then make a well in the centre.
4. Pour your melted butter and treacle mixture into the well, whisking constantly until the butter mixture has combined with the flour, to ensure there are no lumps. Add your milk and egg mixture, then fold in your fresh ginger.
5. Pour into the prepared loaf tin and air fry at 160°C (325°F) for 55 minutes, covering with foil after 25 minutes if the top is starting to catch.
6. Leave to cool in the tin and, if you can bear it, store in an airtight container and wait for a couple of days more before eating! This cake definitely improves with time.
7. If you'd like extra indulgence, make a simple glacé icing by sifting the icing sugar into a bowl and slowly adding citrus juice until you get a thick, glossy icing. Pour over the cake and let it drip down the sides. Let set for a couple of hours before slicing.

CHOCOLATE FONDANTS

Serves. 4

Prep time . . . . . 10 minutes, plus 30 minutes chilling

Bake time . . . . . 11 minutes

Equipment

4 x 100 ml (3½ fl oz) ramekins

For the Fondants

100 g (3½ oz). . . . salted butter, melted

2 teaspoons . . . . unsweetened cocoa powder

100g. . . . . plain dark chocolate, minimum 70% cocoa solids, broken into pieces

60 g (2¼ oz). . . . . self-raising flour

1 . . . . large egg

1 . . . . large egg yolk

50 g (1¾ oz) . . . . . sugar (any)

To serve

Double cream or ice cream and caramel sauce (see page 20 for homemade)

The classic dinner party dessert - and a notoriously difficult one at that! However, the air fryer makes these a doddle and they can be prepped a couple of days ahead and left in the refrigerator (or freezer, see Tip) until you're ready to bake. For a bit of extra indulgence, pop a caramel chocolate or truffle in the middle.

1. Grab your ramekins and brush the inside of each with some of the melted butter. Divide the cocoa between the ramekins and tap it around to coat the insides. (Do this over the rest of the melted butter to catch any excess!)
2. Add the chocolate to the butter and melt again until smooth, then stir in the flour.
3. In a separate bowl, whisk together the egg, egg yolk and sugar. Whisk really well for a few minutes until thicker and lighter. Pour this into the chocolate mixture and stir until completely combined.
4. Pour into your prepared ramekins, level with the back of a teaspoon, then refrigerate for a minimum of 30 minutes (or even overnight).
5. Air fry at 180°C (350°F) for 11 minutes (or 9 minutes if baking just one). Leave to stand for 1 minute before serving. You can either serve these straight in the ramekins or turn them out carefully, using a thick tea towel or oven glove to protect your hands. Delicious with cold double cream or ice cream and a drizzle of caramel sauce.

TIP

- If air frying these straight from frozen, add 4 minutes to the bake time.

MIXED BERRY CRUMBLE

Serves. 4-6

Prep time . . . . . 15 minutes

Bake time . . . . . 45-55 minutes

Equipment

15 or 18 cm (6 or 7 inch) square cake tin (not loose-bottomed), or equivalent sized baking dish/ silicone liner

For the Berries

450 g (1 lb). . . . . . mixed frozen berries

1 tablespoon . . . . caster sugar

1 teaspoon. . . . . . plain flour

For the Topping

60 g (2¼ oz). . . . . plain flour

75 g (2½ oz) . . . . . porridge oats

60 g (2¼ oz). . . . . demerara sugar

¼ teaspoon . . . . . fine salt

60 g (2¼ oz). . . . . cold unsalted butter, cubed

You can't go far wrong with a comforting bowl of warm fruit and buttery crumble. This version uses frozen mixed berries for super-easy prep: no need to get out the chopping board! We like adding oats and demerara sugar to the topping as it gives the crumble such a nubbly, crispy texture.

1. Toss the frozen berries with the caster sugar and flour in the tin or baking dish or liner you've chosen.
2. Air fry at 160°C (325°F) for 15-20 minutes, stirring halfway through, until juicy and bubbling. Use a butter knife to cut any larger pieces of fruit (such as whole strawberries) into smaller pieces.
3. Meanwhile, make the topping by combining the flour, oats, demerara sugar and salt in a medium bowl. Add the butter and rub it into the dry ingredients using your fingertips, until you get a coarse, sandy mixture.
4. Sprinkle this over the cooked fruit in the tin and return to the air fryer for 15 minutes at 150°C (300°F), followed by a final 15-20 minutes at 140°C (275°F), until the crumble is golden and dry on top. Let it cool for a few minutes before serving up.

VICTORIA SPONGE TRAYBAKE

Serves 9

Prep time . . . . . 10 minutes

Bake time . . . . . 55–60 minutes

Equipment

15 cm (6 inch) square cake tin, base and sides greased and lined with a sling of baking paper, secured with metal binder clips (see page 10), foil

For the Cake

150 g (5½ oz) . . . . softened butter, or margarine
150 g (5½ oz) . . . . caster sugar
1 tablespoon . . . . vanilla extract or paste
2 . . . . large eggs
150 g (5½ oz) . . . . self-raising flour
splash . . . . milk
pinch. . . . . icing sugar (optional)
drop . . . . vanilla extract (optional)
150 ml (¼ pint). . . double cream
100 g (3½ oz). . . . raspberry or strawberry jam or Roasted Fruit Compote (see page 21)

To serve

Icing sugar, to dust
Fresh berries, halved if large

While this old-school bake is usually round, most air fryers we've found aren't! To maximize cake space, we've used a square tin to make a traybake; each square just happens to be the perfect portion ready for garden parties galore.

1. In a mixing bowl, beat together the butter, sugar and vanilla until pale and fluffy. Add the eggs one at a time and beat well until combined. Fold in the flour in 2 parts, then add the splash of milk to loosen.
2. Pour into the prepared cake tin, level with the back of a spoon and air fry at 160°C (325°F) for 20 minutes. Cover with foil and bake for another 35–40 minutes, until a toothpick inserted into the centre comes out clean. Leave to cool in the tin for 5 minutes before turning out on to a wire rack to cool completely.
3. Lightly whip the cream (adding a pinch of icing sugar and vanilla extract or paste if you like!) and keep refrigerated until ready to use.
4. When ready to serve, carefully slice your cake in half horizontally to create 2 layers. Add your jam or compote to the base layer and then carefully dollop on two thirds of your whipped cream.
5. Place the other cake layer on top then sift over some icing sugar. Dollop 9 teaspoons of cream over the cake and pop a berry or half on each. Slice into the 9 squares for serving.

PAVLOVA

Serves	8
Prep time	25 minutes, plus overnight resting
Bake time	2 hours

Equipment

15 cm (6 inch) square cake tin, parchment or silicone liners (or baking paper), piping bag (optional)

For the Pavlova

280 g (10 oz)	caster sugar
3	large egg whites (120 g/4 oz)
½	small lemon, juiced
½ teaspoon	cornflour

To serve

150 ml (¼ pint)	double or whipping cream
100 g (3½ oz)	lemon curd, plus an extra 2 tablespoons for drizzling
200 g (7 oz)	mixed fresh or frozen berries
handful	mint leaves

An electric whisk is a must for this! Sadly, muscles just don't quite get the same lift in the egg whites that electric power does... Pile your pavlova high with fresh berries in the summertime or, for a more wintry version, a compote using roasted pears (see page 21) makes the ideal substitute - just drizzle with some salted Cheat's Caramel Sauce (see page 20) instead!

1. Start by adding the sugar to the cake tin, covering with foil and popping in the air fryer at 180°C (350°F) for 8 minutes. Stir the sugar then air fry for a further 5 minutes. We're just trying to heat the sugar here to make it dissolve easily in the egg whites, so don't let it start to caramelize.
2. Add your egg whites to a large bowl or stand mixer bowl and start to whisk on a medium speed.
3. Carefully remove the tin with the sugar from the air fryer, using a thick tea towel to protect your hands, and slowly add the warmed sugar a spoonful at a time to the egg whites, whisking all the time.
4. When all the sugar has been added, increase the speed and continue to whisk for 3-5 minutes until the sugar has dissolved and the meringue is stiff. Add the lemon juice and cornflour and give a final whisk.
5. Line your air fryer, fitted with its crisper plate, with baking paper or a parchment or silicone liner. You can then just spoon on the meringue in a large circle or you can add it to a piping bag and pipe pretty flowers, spirals or lines. Make sure there is a flat centre in the circle so you can pile on your cream and berries later.
6. Air fry at 110°C (240°F) for 30 minutes before reducing the setting to 95°C (200°F) and baking for a further 1½ hours. Turn the air fryer off and then leave the meringue in the drawer overnight.
7. When ready to serve (no longer than an hour before), whip your cream to soft peaks. Swirl the lemon curd through and then add to your pavlova. Pile high with berries, picked mint leaves and an extra drizzle of lemon curd.

4

SOLO ADVENTURES

Craving a single, perfectly formed chocolate chip cookie at 9pm? Look no further. These recipes are for that moment when you really MUST have something sweet but don't want to be standing in the kitchen icing 12 perfect cupcakes.

APPLE CRUMBLE FOR ONE

Serves 1

Prep time . . . . . 10 minutes

Bake time . . . . . 35 minutes

Equipment

1 x 225 g (8 oz) ramekin or equivalent capacity silicone liner, foil

For the Apple Crumble

1 . . . . dessert apple, peeled, cored and diced into 1 cm (½ inch) chunks
1 . . . . teaspoon lemon juice
2 . . . . teaspoons soft light brown sugar
about 20 g (¾ oz) crumbly biscuit of your choice (gingersnaps, shortbread, digestives)
1 teaspoon. . . . . . salted butter
10 g (¼ oz) . . . . . . porridge oats

To serve

Double cream

This nifty little dessert is the perfect way to use up any stale biscuits from your pantry. It works really well with all sorts of crumbly biscuits (we think shortbread or gingersnaps go very nicely with the apple filling). You can of course change up the fruit for something else; just make sure you cut it into roughly 1 cm (½ inch) chunks so the bake time remains similar.

1. Mix the apple, lemon juice and half the sugar in a small bowl, then tip into your ramekin.
2. In the same bowl, crumble your biscuit of choice (or roughly chop it then add to the bowl). Add the butter, oats and remaining sugar, then rub everything together with your fingertips.
3. Scatter the topping over the fruit then cover the ramekin tightly with foil and air fry at 180°C (350°F) for 30 minutes. Remove the foil and air fry for a final 5 minutes so the topping can crisp up and caramelize. Serve with double cream for pouring.

VARIATIONS

- Add 25 g (1 oz) blackberries in with the apples for an autumnal apple-blackberry crumble.
- Use 120 g (4 oz) frozen fruit (e.g. blueberries, forest fruits) instead of the apple.
- Add ¼ teaspoon of ground cinnamon to the fruit, for a cosy flavour.

SINGLE CHOCOLATE CHIP COOKIE

Serves 1

Prep time . . . . . 10 minutes

Bake time . . . . . 7–10 minutes

Equipment

foil

For the Cookie

10 g (¼ oz) . . . . . . unsalted butter, melted

1 teaspoon. . . . . . soft light brown sugar

10 g (¼ oz) . . . . . . golden syrup, maple syrup or runny honey

½ teaspoon . . . . . milk

¼ teaspoon . . . . . vanilla extract

pinch. . . . . fine salt

15 g (½ oz) . . . . . . plain flour

pinch. . . . . bicarbonate of soda

15 g (½ oz) . . . . . . dark chocolate chips or roughly chopped plain dark chocolate

Sometimes you have one of those days where you just need a single, warm chocolate chip cookie, ASAP! Though you can easily double the ingredients if you'd rather make two...

1. In a small bowl, combine the melted butter, sugar, syrup or honey, milk, vanilla and salt until smooth.
2. Add the flour and bicarbonate of soda, stirring to get a soft dough. Stir in the chocolate chips or chopped chocolate.
3. Fit the air fryer with its crisper plate and line with foil.
4. Form the dough into a ball, place in the lined air fryer and air fry at 160°C (325°F) for 7–10 minutes until the edges are set but the middle is still slightly gooey.
5. Let the cookie cool on the foil for 5–10 minutes before removing, as this gives it time to firm up a bit before you can eat it!

CINNAMON DOUGHNUT BITES

Serves 1–2

Prep time . . . . . 10 minutes

Bake time . . . . . 10–12 minutes

Equipment

baking paper

For the Doughnut Bites

65 g (2¼ oz) . . . . . full-fat Greek yogurt
50 g (1¾ oz) . . . . . self-raising flour, plus extra for dusting
pinch. . . . . fine salt
10 g (¼ oz) . . . . . . salted butter, melted
1 tablespoon . . . . caster sugar
¼ teaspoon . . . . . ground cinnamon

This easy yogurt dough doesn't require any yeast, meaning you can mix it up and cook it almost immediately. The chewy little nuggets of dough are air fried, then rolled in salted butter and cinnamon-sugar to impart the flavour of a freshly fried doughnut.

1. Place the yogurt, flour and salt in a medium bowl and mix together to get a soft dough. Knead gently in the bowl until it forms a ball, then set aside to rest for 5 minutes.
2. On a lightly floured work surface, roll the dough out into a snake around 3 cm (1¼ inches) thick. Cut into 8 evenly sized pieces and roll each piece into a ball.
3. Fit the air fryer with its crisper plate and line with a square of baking paper. Add the dough balls and air fry at 150°C (300°F) for 10–12 minutes until golden on top.
4. Transfer the doughnut balls to a bowl and pour over the melted butter, stirring to coat.
5. Combine the sugar and cinnamon in a small bowl and tip this over the doughnut bites, mixing to coat. Serve warm!

MINI HAZELNUT BROWNIE

Serves 1

Prep time . . . . . 5 minutes

Bake time . . . . . 7–10 minutes

Equipment

1 x 85 g (3 oz) ramekin or 1 x 100 ml (3½ fl oz) silicone muffin case

For the Brownie

40 g (1½ oz) . . . . . chocolate-hazelnut spread
1 large . . . . egg yolk
pinch. . . . . fine salt
15 g (½ oz) . . . . . . plain flour

This magical recipe takes advantage of the fact that chocolate-hazelnut spread already contains cocoa, sugar and fat, meaning all you need to add is an egg yolk and some flour to turn it into a brownie! It's best to leave this a little soft in the centre for the perfect texture.

1. In a small bowl, mix the chocolate-hazelnut spread with the egg yolk and salt until smooth. Mix in the flour until fully combined.
2. Scrape the mixture into the ramekin or silicone case and air fry at 150°C (300°F) for 7–10 minutes until the top is slightly shiny, the edges are set but the middle is still soft.
3. Let cool for 5 minutes before digging in.

ROASTED BANANA BOATS

Serves 2

Prep time . . . . . 5 minutes

Bake time . . . . . 15–20 minutes

Equipment

foil

For the Banana Boats

2 . . . . ripe bananas, in their skins

2 teaspoons . . . . peanut butter (or your favourite nut butter) or 2 teaspoons caramel sauce (see page 20 for homemade), optional

30 g (1 oz) . . . . . . dark or milk chocolate chips or buttons (or your favourite chocolate, roughly chopped)

2 tablespoons . . . chopped nuts or 2 of your favourite biscuits, crumbled

To serve

Whipped cream or ice cream (optional)

These are a bit of a blast from the past for both of us! They were always a classic thing our parents would make for us as kids after a barbecue – they are usually cooked on the cooling coals of the grill after you're done with cooking your main meal. However, they work just as well in an air fryer, meaning you can indulge in a soft, gooey banana with melted chocolate chips any time you want.

1. Wash the bananas in their skins. Cut a slit into the skin of each banana, open them up a bit and stuff with the nut butter or caramel sauce, if using. Stuff with the chocolate chips, then wrap each banana individually in a square of foil.
2. Air fry at 200°C (400°F) for 15–20 minutes, until the bananas are meltingly soft.
3. Carefully unwrap and serve, sprinkled with the chopped nuts or crumbled biscuits, with a spoon to scoop straight out of the skins. Add a dollop of whipped cream or some ice cream if you're so inclined.

STICKY TOFFEE PUDDING FOR ONE

Serves. 1

Prep time . . . . . 15 minutes

Bake time . . . . . 15–20 minutes

Equipment

1 x 225 g (8 oz) ramekin

For the Puddings

25 g (1 oz). . . . . . . pitted dates
2 teaspoons . . . . soft dark brown sugar
2 teaspoons . . . . vegetable oil
1 . . . . large egg yolk
2 tablespoons . . . self-raising flour
⅛ teaspoon . . . . . bicarbonate of soda

For the Sauce

1 tablespoon . . . . soft dark brown sugar
1 tablespoon . . . . double cream
2 tablespoons . . . boiling water
pinch. . . . . fine salt

To serve

Vanilla ice cream or double cream

This mini sticky toffee pudding makes its own toffee sauce as it bakes, meaning all you have to do is top it off with some vanilla ice cream or double cream and you're all set to dig straight in!

1. Chop each date with a pair of scissors into around 4 pieces. Place in a small heatproof bowl, cover with boiling water and leave to soak for 5–10 minutes until softened, then drain. Return to the bowl and mash with the back of a fork into a rough paste.
2. Mix the sugar, oil and egg yolk into the mashed dates. Add the flour and bicarbonate of soda then stir until fully combined.
3. Place the sugar for the sauce in the base of the ramekin. Pour over the cream and boiling water, add the salt and stir to combine.
4. Spoon the batter over the sauce and carefully place inside a slightly larger tin (to catch any drips). Air fry at 160°C (325°C) for 15–20 minutes until a toothpick inserted into the centre comes out clean.
5. Let it cool in the ramekin for a few minutes before turning out on to a plate (or you can eat it straight out the ramekin, if you prefer). Serve with a scoop of vanilla ice cream or a drizzle of double cream on top, if you fancy.

TWO BLUEBERRY MUFFINS

Serves. 2

Prep time . . . . . 15 minutes

Bake time . . . . . 14–18 minutes

Equipment

2 x 225 g (8 oz) ramekins

For the Muffins

20 g (¾ oz). . . . . . salted butter, melted

1 tablespoon . . . . semi-skimmed or whole milk

1 . . . . large egg white

1½ tablespoons . . granulated, caster or soft light brown sugar

¼ teaspoon . . . . . vanilla extract

pinch. . . . . fine salt

40 g (1½ oz) . . . . . self-raising flour

70 g (2½ oz) . . . . . frozen blueberries

¼ teaspoon . . . . . ground cinnamon

Baking up a couple of warm blueberry muffins in your air fryer is the perfect way to start the weekend – one for now, one for tomorrow! We like to warm the frozen blueberries up first, so they get juicy and soft before being covered with batter. We found that baking these muffins in paper cases resulted in soggy bottoms, so we use ramekins here to combat that.

1. In a small bowl, mix the melted butter, milk, egg white, 1 tablespoon of the sugar, the vanilla and salt. Sift in the flour and mix until you have a smooth batter.
2. Divide the blueberries between the ramekins and air fry at 160°C (325°F) for 3–5 minutes until softened and starting to release some of their juice.
3. In a small bowl, combine the remaining sugar with the cinnamon.
4. Divide the batter between the ramekins, sprinkle with the cinnamon-sugar and return to the air fryer for 14–18 minutes, until a toothpick inserted into the centre of a muffin comes out with no batter attached (be mindful the bottom will be a bit wetter due to the blueberries).
5. Remove from the air fryer and allow to cool for 5 minutes before eating with a spoon, straight from the ramekin.

TIP

- If you want to bake one now and one tomorrow, let the second ramekin of roasted blueberries cool before topping with batter. Refrigerate overnight. When ready to eat, air fry at 160°C (325°F) for 18–22 minutes, until a toothpick inserted into the centre of a muffin comes out clean.

WEEKDAY COOKIES

Makes 5–8

Prep time . . . . . 5 minutes, plus chilling

Bake time . . . . . 10–12 minutes

Equipment

2 parchment or silicone liners

For the Cookies

150 g (5½ oz) . . . . porridge oats
50 g (1¾ oz) . . . . . wholemeal flour
1 teaspoon. . . . . . ground cinnamon
30 g (1 oz) . . . . . . pumpkin seeds
30 g (1 oz) . . . . . . dried mixed peel
30 g (1 oz) . . . . . . raisins
2. . . . . really ripe bananas
2. . . . . tablespoons honey
1 . . . . large egg
2 tablespoons . . . nut butter (optional)

These cookies are the perfect weekday treat - with no refined sugar, they are great for a midday snack, after the gym or just on the bus on the way to see friends. You can make 5 big ones to keep you going Monday to Friday, or you can make them slightly smaller to keep the fun going until Sunday! You can easily replace the raisins with dried mango and the mixed peel with desiccated coconut for a tropical vibe.

1. In a large bowl, mix together the oats, flour and cinnamon. Fold through the pumpkin seeds, mixed peel and raisins.
2. In another bowl, mash the bananas and combine with the honey and egg to make a smooth paste. Add the nut butter, if using.
3. Add your wet ingredients to your dry and mix well to make a dough. Use an ice-cream scoop to scoop your cookies onto your 2 liners and press down to create even shapes. Refrigerate for 10–15 minutes.
4. Air fry one batch at 160°C (325°F) for 10–12 minutes (if you made 5 larger cookies, they will take nearer the 12-minute mark). This gives them a perfectly crunchy top and gooey middle but if you like them crunchy all the way through, flip them over and air fry for a further 4 minutes.
5. Leave to cool on the liner while you bake the second batch, then let them cool completely on a wire rack.

TIP

- You can also keep the cookies, scooped on their liners in the refrigerator (in a covered container), and bake one batch on Sunday and the other on Wednesday. They last for 3 days as cookie dough and a further 3 days when baked.

PEA & PARMESAN PERSONAL FRITTATA

Serves. 1

Prep time . . . . . 5 minutes

Bake time . . . . . 20–25 minutes

Equipment

13–15 cm (5–6 inch) ceramic baking dish

For the Frittata

1 teaspoon. . . . . . olive oil
50 g (1¾ oz) . . . . . frozen petits pois
2 . . . . hash browns (defrosted if frozen), broken up, or 3 cooked new potatoes (can be canned), sliced
3 . . . . large eggs
30 g (1 oz) . . . . . . Parmesan cheese, grated
few stalks each . . flat leaf parsley and mint
pinch. . . . . salt and pepper

The air fryer takes all the guesswork (and flip work!) out of the classic frittata, which makes this easy breakfast or lunch even easier, if that's possible... Any veg works here, so use whatever's going a bit limp in the refrigerator, or leftovers from other meals.

1. Add the olive oil to your baking dish with the petits pois and either the hash browns or potatoes. Season with salt and pepper then air fry at 160°C (325°F) for 5 minutes.
2. Beat the eggs well in a jug and whisk in the grated Parmesan. Use scissors to snip the herbs in and mix well. Open the air fryer drawer and pour the egg mixture over the peas and potatoes.
3. Increase the temperature to 170°C (340°F) and bake for 15–20 minutes until set. When cooked, you can either turn out of the baking dish carefully with a tea towel to protect your hands, or eat straight from it. A fresh green salad on the side is ideal!

TWO LOVELY CRUSTY ROLLS

Makes 2

Prep time . . . . . 10 minutes, plus 2 hours proving

Bake time . . . . . 18–20 minutes

Equipment

baking paper

For the Rolls

125 g (4½ oz) . . . . strong white flour
2 g (¾ teaspoon) . fast-action dried yeast
¼ teaspoon . . . . . fine salt
¼ teaspoon . . . . . sugar
100 ml (3½ fl oz). . warm milk or water

To finish

splash . . . . olive oil
splash . . . . milk, for brushing
sprinkle . . . . seeds, such as sesame, poppy or flax, to sprinkle (optional)

TIP

- These keep really well to be refreshed the next day for 2–3 minutes in the air fryer at 170°C (350°C).

Is there anything better than the smell of fresh bread? Maybe crunching through a perfect crust to get to it... These two little rolls are the ideal lunch, so make your dough first thing and by 1pm you'll have the perfect vessel for all manner of fillings.

1. Combine all the dry ingredients in a mixing bowl and add the liquid slowly, stirring until no loose flour remains. Turn out onto the work surface and knead for 5–6 minutes until the dough comes together a bit more and looks smooth.
2. Pop back in the bowl with a drizzle of olive oil to grease, cover with clingfilm or a damp tea towel and leave in a warm place for an hour or until it has risen to double its size.
3. When risen, split the dough into 2 equal pieces and pinch the pieces into themselves to form 2 tight balls. Place pinched side down on the work surface and cup your hand over. Scoop the balls around with your hand clasped over them to form tight rolls.
4. Line your air fryer basket with a piece of baking paper, then place the rolls directly on top. Cover again in a warm place for another hour until well risen again.
5. When ready to bake, brush the tops with a little milk and slash the tops with scissors or a knife to make a little cross, if you like. If you're using them, you can sprinkle the rolls with seeds.
6. Air fry at 160°C (325°F) for 15 minutes until golden brown and then flip over and bake for a further 3–5 minutes. They are cooked when a tap on the bottom sounds hollow.

5

TEATIME TREATS

The ritual of teatime is deliciously comforting: a cup of tea in one hand, a warm bun in the other. Forget about dusty biscuits from a tin, we're here to show you how to whip up a gorgeous homemade bake in no time. You'll never buy supermarket cookies again!

LEMON TARTS

Makes 4–5

Prep time . . . . . 30 minutes, plus cooling

Bake time . . . . . 38–42 minutes

Equipment

4 or 5 small (10 cm/4 inch) tart tins

For the Tarts

1 quantity . . . . . . Sweet Shortcrust Pastry (see page 18)
1 . . . . large egg
75 g (2½ oz) . . . . . caster sugar
80 ml (2¾ fl oz) . . double cream
2 . . . . large lemons, 1 finely zested and both juiced (50 ml/2 fl oz juice)

To serve

Icing sugar and crème fraîche (optional)

This may be a classic recipe but don't be afraid to change up your citrus – it works so well with lime or grapefruit too! If you want a little extra sweetness, use half the meringue recipe from our Pavlova (see page 66): swoop it on with a spoon and blowtorch for a final flourish. You can also bake this as a big tart, if you like, by following the baking instructions for the Custard Tart on page 128.

1. Start by rolling out your pastry until it is the thickness of a pound coin (3 mm/⅛ inch). Cut circles of pastry a little larger than your tins and line them gently, pushing the pastry into each corner carefully. Refrigerate for 30 minutes.
2. Remove them from the refrigerator and line each with a piece of baking paper. Fill with baking beans or uncooked rice and air fry at 160°C (325°F) for 10 minutes. Carefully remove the beans or rice and baking paper and air fry for a further 5–8 minutes until light golden brown on the base.
3. Meanwhile, in a jug, whisk together the egg, sugar, cream, lemon zest and juice.
4. Pour the lemon cream into the baked tart cases, then cover with the base of a loose-bottomed cake tin and air fry at 140°C (275°F) for 20 minutes, then remove the cake tin base and bake for a further 3–4 minutes. They might still have a wobble in the middle but will set as they cool.
5. Leave to cool in the air fryer basket for 20 minutes, then carefully remove and cool for a further hour in the tins.
6. Serve with a sprinkling of icing sugar and a dollop of crème fraîche (or some extra double cream), if you like.

CHOCOLATE PEANUT BUTTER SNACK CAKE

Serves. 9

Prep time . . . . . 20 minutes

Bake time . . . . . 25–30 minutes

Equipment

15 cm (6 inch) square cake tin, base and sides lined with a sling of baking paper, secured with metal binder clips (see page 10)

For the Cake

90 g (3¼ oz). . . . . smooth, creamy peanut butter
60 g (2¼ oz). . . . . soft light brown sugar
35 g (1¼ oz) . . . . . unsalted butter, softened
1 . . . . large egg
2 tablespoons . . . water
60 g (2¼ oz). . . . . self-raising flour

For the Topping

40 ml (1½ fl oz). . . double cream
75 g (2½ oz) . . . . . milk chocolate chips
50 g (1¾ oz) . . . . . smooth, creamy peanut butter
25 g (1 oz). . . . . . . roasted, salted peanuts

If you like chocolate peanut butter cups, this is the cake for you! A soft peanut butter sponge is topped with a layer of creamy peanut butter and milk chocolate ganache. The simple decoration of chocolate chips and salted peanuts is faff-free and delicious. Slice into squares and snack away.

1. Make the cake batter by creaming together the peanut butter, sugar and softened butter in a medium bowl, until smooth and light. Beat in the egg and water, then fold in the flour.
2. Scrape the batter into the prepared cake tin, spread out into an even layer and air fry at 160°C (325°F) for 20 minutes, then reduce the temperature to 150°C (300°F) and air fry for a further 5–10 minutes. The cake is done when well risen and a toothpick inserted into the centre of the cake comes out clean.
3. Let the cake cool in the tin for 10 minutes before inverting on to a wire rack, letting it cool upside down.
4. Meanwhile, make the ganache by warming the cream in a small pan on the stove until gently steaming. Remove from the heat and stir in 50 g (1¾ oz) of the chocolate chips. Set aside for 5 minutes so the chocolate can melt fully, then stir until smooth. Let cool to room temperature.
5. Spread the peanut butter over the cooled cake, then spread the cooled ganache on top. Decorate with the remaining chocolate chips and the peanuts, then cut into 9 squares and serve.

PISTACHIO PROFITEROLES

Makes 12–15

Prep time . . . . . 15 minutes, plus chilling

Bake time . . . . . 25 minutes

Equipment

piping bag fitted with round nozzle

For the Profiteroles

1 quantity . . . . . . Choux Pastry (see page 19)
150 g (5½ oz) . . . . white chocolate
¼ teaspoon . . . . . rosewater (optional)
200 ml (7 fl oz) . . . double cream
100 g (3½ oz) . . . . pistachio paste
50 g (1¾ oz) . . . . . shelled unsalted pistachios, chopped

Since we were both little, our favourite gelato flavour has always been (and will always be!) pistachio. While we haven't mastered gelato in an air fryer, these profiteroles work super well. Hunting down pistachio paste is a must here – unless you're a fan of making your own nut butters! Most Italian delis will sell a version of it, or it's readily available online. Once you've tried it, you'll find a hundred uses for it – or just eat it straight from the spoon…

1. Follow the choux pastry instructions on page 19 to make and bake your profiteroles. Depending on the size of your fryer basket you may need to bake your buns in 2–3 batches, about 5 per batch.
2. Melt the white chocolate in a small heatproof and microwave-safe bowl in the microwave in 20-second bursts until smooth. Stir through the rosewater, if using, then let cool to room temperature.
3. Add the cream and pistachio paste to a large mixing bowl and whip to soft peaks. Add to the piping bag.
4. Take your profiteroles and either use a sharp knife to cut a hole in the bottom or just slice in half. Pipe some pistachio cream in each, then chill for 20 minutes.
5. Dip or drizzle the white chocolate over each and then sprinkle over the chopped pistachios. Refrigerate to set for 20 minutes before digging in!

SPECULOOS CHEESECAKE BARS

Makes . . . . 8 bars or 9 squares

Prep time . . . . . 20 minutes, plus 6 hours chilling

Bake time . . . . . 18–22 minutes

Equipment

15 or 18 cm (6 or 7 inch) square cake tin, base and sides lined with a sling of baking paper, secured with metal binder clips (see page 10)

For the Bars

12 . . . . caramelized speculoos biscuits, such as Biscoff

40 g (1½ oz) . . . . . unsalted butter, melted

280 g (10 oz) . . . . full-fat cream cheese

30 g (1 oz) . . . . . . soft light brown sugar

1 . . . . large egg

200 g (7 oz). . . . . caramelized biscuit spread, such as Biscoff (smooth or crunchy)

50 g (1¾ oz) . . . . . double cream

Those iconic caramelized Belgian biscuits incorporate seamlessly into these rich, golden cheesecake bars. We use the crushed biscuits in the base plus the spread in the cheesecake mix, for maximum caramelized flavour. For decoration, a simple layer of spread gives these bars a sleek appearance, but you can go a step further by adorning each one with a dollop of whipped cream and a whole biscuit.

1. Place the biscuits in a sandwich bag and crush with a rolling pin until you get a fine crumb. Add to a small bowl and mix with the melted butter, then tip into the prepared tin and press down into an even layer.
2. In a medium bowl, cream together the cream cheese and sugar. Mix in the egg, followed by 150 g (5½ oz) of the caramelized biscuit spread and the cream, mixing until smooth.
3. Pour this mixture over the biscuit base and air fry at 160°C (325°F) for 18–22 minutes until browned in places, the edges are set and the middle is still a tad wobbly when you shake the tin (if you have a digital thermometer, the middle should have reached 63–65°C/145–149°F).
4. Turn off the air fryer and leave the cheesecake in there with the drawer shut so it can gradually cool down for 30 minutes.
5. Warm up the remaining caramelized biscuit spread in the microwave or a heatproof bowl set over a pan of simmering water. You just want it to melt until runny. Pour this over the cheesecake in the tin and refrigerate for at least 6 hours so it can fully set.
6. Remove the cheesecake from the tin and use a sharp knife to cut into 8 bars, or 9 squares.

TRIPLE CHOCOLATE SHARING COOKIE

Serves 4–6

Prep time . . . . . 15 minutes

Bake time . . . . . 10–15 minutes

Equipment

15 cm (6 inch) round baking dish or cake tin

For the Cookie

40 g (1½ oz) . . . . . salted butter
50 g (1¾ oz) . . . . . plain dark chocolate, 70% cocoa solids
50 g (1¾ oz) . . . . . soft light brown sugar
2 tablespoons . . . unsweetened cocoa powder
1 . . . . large egg
60 g (2¼ oz) . . . . . plain flour
¼ teaspoon . . . . . bicarbonate of soda
100 g (3½ oz) . . . . mixed chocolate chips or roughly chopped chocolate (milk, white or dark, or a mixture)

Instead of making individual cookies, bake up your cookie dough in a single dish so it ends up with crispy edges and a gooey middle. This is the perfect low-effort dessert to share with friends; just serve it up warm with a scoop of ice cream and let everyone dig in.

1. Melt the butter and chocolate together, either in the microwave or in a heatproof bowl set over a pot of simmering water, then remove from the heat. Let cool so it's only just warm.
2. Stir in the sugar, cocoa powder and egg until smooth, then mix in the flour and bicarbonate of soda until you get a soft dough. Finally, stir in the chocolate chips.
3. Press the cookie dough into the baking dish and air fry at 160°C (325°F) for 10–15 minutes until it looks set on top and a toothpick inserted into the centre comes out with some sticky crumbs attached.
4. Let it cool for 10 minutes before digging in, with or without a scoop of vanilla ice cream on top!

TIP

- To make this ahead of time, prep the cookie dough and press into the baking dish you're using. Cover and refrigerate until you're ready to bake (up to 5 days). Air fry for an extra 5–10 minutes.

MALTED MILLIONAIRE'S SHORTBREAD

Makes . . . . 9 large or 16 small squares

Prep time . . . . . 30 minutes, plus cooling

Bake time . . . . . 25-30 minutes

Equipment

15 cm (6 inch) square cake tin, lined with a sling of baking paper, secured with metal binder clips (see page 10)

For the Shortbread base

100 g (3½ oz). . . . plain flour
65 g (2¼ oz) . . . . . cold unsalted butter, cubed
20 g (¾ oz). . . . . . soft light brown sugar
20 g (¾ oz). . . . . . malted milk powder
¼ teaspoon . . . . . fine salt

For the Caramel

½ x 397 g (14 oz) . . can condensed milk
35 g (1¼ oz) . . . . . malted milk powder
75 g (2½ oz) . . . . . unsalted butter
65 g (2¼ oz) . . . . . granulated sugar
25 g (1 oz). . . . . . . golden syrup
¼ teaspoon . . . . . fine salt

For the Topping

80 g (3 oz) . . . . . . malted chocolate balls
150 g (5½ oz) . . . . dark chocolate, melted and cooled
½ teaspoon . . . . . vegetable oil

How could something as iconic as millionaire's shortbread get even better? With a touch of moreish malted milk powder mixed into the shortbread base and chewy caramel layer - that's how! The combination is utterly mouthwatering and even better when filled with crunchy chocolate malt balls, too.

1. Make the shortbread base by combining the ingredients in a medium bowl. Use your fingertips to rub the butter into the dry ingredients until you get a crumbly mixture.
2. Press this mixture into the prepared cake tin. Air fry at 160°C (325°F) for 10 minutes until golden but still soft, then reduce the setting to 140°C (275°F) and air fry for a further 15-20 minutes until deep golden all over and firm. Remove from the air fryer and set aside to cool.
3. Make the caramel by whisking the condensed milk with the malted milk powder and 2 tablespoons water in a medium pan, until fully combined. Add the butter, sugar, golden syrup and salt then cook over a low heat, stirring constantly until the butter has melted.
4. Now turn the heat up to medium-high so it starts to bubble, and keep stirring the caramel until it thickens and turns a deep caramel colour, 10-15 minutes. You need to make sure you're scraping the pan as you stir to prevent the caramel catching and burning.
5. Pour the hot caramel over the shortbread base in the tin and leave to cool at room temperature for 30-45 minutes, until cooled but still soft.
6. Push the malted chocolate balls into the top of the cooled caramel. Mix the melted, cooled chocolate with the oil and pour over the malted balls, spreading it out into an even layer.
7. Chill until fully set, then remove from the tin and use a hot, sharp knife to cut into 9 large or 16 small squares.

SMALL BATCH CINNAMON ROLLS

Makes	4
Prep time	30 minutes, plus 30 minutes proving
Bake time	12–15 minutes

Equipment

15 or 18 cm (6 or 7 inch) square or round cake tin, greased and lined (if using a loose-bottomed tin, scrunch up a piece of baking paper that's a bit larger than your tin, un-scrunch it and then use it to line the base and sides of the tin),

For the Rolls

½ quantity	Bread Dough (see page 16), made using melted butter not oil
25 g (1 oz)	unsalted butter, softened
35 g (1¼ oz)	soft dark brown sugar
½ tablespoon	ground cinnamon
pinch	fine salt

Izy has been obsessed with cinnamon rolls since she started baking as a teenager, and this small batch is perfect for when a craving hits! You can easily veganize these by using a plant-based butter in the dough and filling, too. They're best the day they're made, but you can freshen them back up in the air fryer for a few minutes at 180°C (350°F) in the subsequent days.

1. Prepare the bread dough according to the recipe on page 16.
2. Mix the softened butter, sugar, cinnamon and salt in a small bowl until smooth and very soft (you can add around ½ tablespoon hot water to help soften it a bit).
3. Tip the risen dough out on to a clean work surface and dust lightly with flour. Roll out into a rectangle roughly 18 x 25 cm (7 x 10 inches). Dot the filling over and spread out to cover the entire surface of the dough.
4. Starting at one of the short edges, roll the dough up into a Swiss roll. Cut into 4 equal pieces and place cut side up into the prepared tin.
5. Cover with a clean tea towel and leave somewhere warm to prove until almost doubled in volume, 20–30 minutes.
6. Air fry at 180°C (350°F) for 12–15 minutes until well browned and caramelized. Let them cool for a few minutes before eating.

JAM TART BARS

Makes 8

Prep time . . . . . 15 minutes, plus 20 minutes chilling

Bake time . . . . . 30–35 minutes

Equipment

18 cm (7 inch) square, loose-bottomed cake tin, greased and base lined, or square silicone liner

For the Jam Tart Bars

1 quantity . . . . . . Sweet Shortcrust Pastry (see page 18)

300 g (10½ oz). . . your favourite jam, or 1 quantity Roasted Fruit Compote (see page 21)

You don't need to fall down a rabbit hole to enjoy these bars - they're ready from start to finish in under an hour, so are the perfect treat to make last minute with things you probably have in your cupboard.

1. Divide your pastry into 2 portions, one third and two thirds. Roll the larger portion out to the thickness of a pound coin (3 mm/⅛ inch) and use to line your cake tin or silicone liner with a small border up the sides. Prick the base with a fork, then chill for 20 minutes.
2. Meanwhile, roll out the smaller pastry portion to the same thickness and cut out little shapes, or make strips with a pizza cutter if you'd like a lattice effect over the bars. Set aside.
3. When your pastry has chilled, line it with baking paper or clingfilm then fill with baking beans or uncooked rice. Air fry at 160°C (325°F) for 12 minutes, then carefully remove the beans or rice and baking paper and air fry for further 8–9 minutes until light golden brown on the base.
4. Spread your jam or compote over the pastry then pop your little shapes on top of your jammy base.
5. Air fry at 180°C (350°F) for 10–12 minutes until the pastry pieces on top are golden brown and the jam or compote is bubbling a little.
6. Leave to cool completely in the tin or liner before turning out carefully and cutting into 8 bars.

WHIPPED LEMON & RASPBERRY CREAM BUNS

Makes 6

Prep time . . . . . 20 minutes, plus 3–4 hours proving

Bake time . . . . . 20–24 minutes

Equipment

parchment or silicone liner

For the Buns

50 ml (2 fl oz) . . . . double cream, at room temperature
50 ml (2 fl oz) . . . . milk, at room temperature
1 . . . . lemon, finely zested
2 . . . . medium eggs
20 g (¾ oz) . . . . . . caster sugar
140 g (5 oz) . . . . . strong white flour
50 g (1¾ oz) . . . . . plain flour
1 teaspoon . . . . . . fast-action dried yeast
splash . . . . vegetable oil

For the Sugar Syrup

1 tablespoon . . . . caster sugar
1 tablespoon . . . . hot water

For the Filling

300 ml (½ pint) . . double cream
3 tablespoons . . . icing sugar
1 . . . . large lemon (or 2 small), finely zested
200 g (7 oz) . . . . . raspberries

You can use a stand mixer if you wish, but this recipe is so lovely and soft to knead with your hands! It takes a little longer to rise as it is an enriched cream dough. These are also amazing with a scoop of ice cream in instead of the whipped cream filling, so get creative in the summer months!

1. Measure the cream and milk together in a measuring jug (if not at room temperature you can sit this in a bowl of hot water for 10 minutes, or blast in the microwave for 30 seconds). Whisk in the lemon zest, one of the eggs and the sugar until combined.
2. Add the flours and yeast to a large mixing bowl and whisk to combine. Make a well in the centre and pour in the cream mixture. Mix well, then turn out on to the work surface. Add a little more flour if too sticky and knead for 8–10 minutes, or until the dough is smooth and springs back when poked.
3. Brush a little vegetable oil around the sides of the mixing bowl and add the dough back in. Cover and leave in a warm place for a couple of hours or until doubled in size.
4. When the dough is ready, knock it back to remove the air bubbles then split evenly into 6 pieces. Roll each piece into a round or oblong bun. Cover and leave to rise once more for 1–1½ hours, or until doubled again.
5. Add yourbuns to the air fryer, directly on the crisper plate. Whisk the remaining egg and use to brush the buns. Air fry at 160°C (325°F) for 20–24 minutes until dark golden. While the buns are baking, make your sugar syrup by dissolving the sugar in the hot water. Set aside.
6. Remove the buns carefully from the air fryer, using tongs, then brush over the sugar syrup while they're still warm. Let them cool for a couple of hours.
7. Meanwhile, whip the cream with the icing sugar to soft peaks. Mix through the lemon zest then add the raspberries and stir through the cream to make berry swirls.
8. Slice the buns down the middle until near the bottom (don't split all the way!) Divide the berry cream between the buns and use the back of a knife or spoon to smooth it down so it's flush with the buns.

SIMPLE SCONES

Makes 4

Prep time . . . . . 10 minutes

Bake time . . . . . 13–15 minutes

Equipment

parchment or silicone liner, plain 6 cm (2½ inch) cookie cutter or glass

For the Scones

200 g (7 oz) . . . . . self-raising flour, plus extra for dusting

1 teaspoon. . . . . . baking powder

25 g (1 oz). . . . . . . caster sugar

50 g (1¾ oz) . . . . . unsalted butter, softened

1 . . . . large egg

about 100 ml. . . . milk, (3½ fl oz) plus extra to glaze

For the Optional Mix-ins

50 g (1¾ oz) . . . . . sultanas or blueberries or 40 g (1½ oz) chocolate chips or glacé cherries

Growing up, a Sunday afternoon in Dom's house wasn't complete without a plate of her Dad's scones and two little bowls of jam and cream on the side. And she wonders where she got her sweet tooth from? This recipe couldn't be easier and you can personalize your scones to suit your tastes with blueberries, chocolate or cherries!

1. Start by adding the flour, baking powder and sugar to a large mixing bowl. Add the butter then mix with a knife until the butter is evenly distributed throughout the flour.
2. Add your egg to a measuring jug and beat. Pour in enough milk to make up to 150 ml (¼ pint) of liquid then add to the dry ingredients.
3. Keep using the knife to stir until just combined, then turn out on to the work surface. Add any mix-ins here and gently squish into the dough.
4. Using your hands dusted with a bit of flour, pat the dough into a very thick, rough square. They don't rise much so make them as thick as you'd like!
5. Using the cookie cutter or a glass the same size, cut 4 scones out of the dough. Re-pat the dough carefully if you need to use it all up.
6. Add to your air fryer basket and brush on a little extra milk for a shiny top – do not let the milk run down the sides or it will inhibit the rise. Air fry at 200°C (400°F) for 10–12 minutes, until golden brown, then flip them over and bake upside down for a further 3 minutes.

JAMMY PLUM CAKE

Serves. 6

Prep time . . . . . 15 minutes

Bake time . . . . . 35–45 minutes

Equipment

18 cm (7 inch) round cake tin, lined, greased and floured

For the Cake

60 g (2¼ oz). . . . . unsalted butter, softened
100 g (3½ oz). . . . caster sugar
¼ teaspoon . . . . . fine salt
1 . . . . large egg
110 g (3¾ oz) . . . . self-raising flour
80 ml (2¾ fl oz) . . milk (cows' or plant-based)

For the Jammy Plums

300 g (10½ oz). . . plums (about 5), pitted and cut into 3 cm (1¼ inch) chunks
30 g (1 oz) . . . . . . caster sugar
1 tablespoon . . . . lemon juice

Sometimes mixing fresh fruit into cakes can lead to a watered-down flavour and mushy texture - not ideal! By roasting plums before swirling them into a buttery cake batter, their flavour is concentrated and their texture becomes less squishy. As a bonus, whatever plum syrup forms as the fruit roasts can be spooned over the cooked cake for an extra dimension of sticky sweetness.

1. Mix the plums with the sugar and lemon juice in a small roasting dish or silicone liner that fits in your air fryer. Air fry at 160°C (325°F) for 10–15 minutes, stirring halfway, until they are looking jammy. Set aside.
2. Make the cake batter by creaming the butter, sugar and salt in a medium bowl until smooth and fluffy. Mix in the egg followed by the flour and milk to get a smooth batter.
3. Pour into the lined cake tin then scatter the roasted plums on top, reserving any fruity syrup from the roasting dish for later. Push the plums into the batter a bit then air fry at 160°C (325°F) for 25–30 minutes until golden. When a toothpick is inserted into the centre of the cake, it comes out clean.
4. Let cool in the tin for 10 minutes before turning out onto a wire rack and pouring over any of the plum syrup you reserved. Leave to cool completely before slicing and serving.

RHUBARB CUSTARD CREAM BARS

Makes 9

Prep time . . . . . 15 minutes

Bake time . . . . . 17–22 minutes

Equipment

15 cm (6 inch) square cake tin, base and sides lined with a sling of baking paper, secured with metal binder clips (see page 10)

For the Bars

200 g (7 oz) . . . . . custard creams, or other vanilla sandwich cookies
35 g (1¼ oz) . . . . . butter, melted
10 g (½ oz) . . . . . . custard powder (not instant)
60 g (2¼ oz) . . . . . caster sugar
100 ml (3½ fl oz). . double cream
1 . . . . large egg
200 g (7 oz) . . . . . rhubarb compote (see page 21), cooled

The combination of rhubarb and custard is a match made in heaven. A buttery topping made from crushed custard creams finishes a whisked-together custard and a rhubarb compote. We use a little bit of custard powder in the mix to give it that nostalgic, heady vanilla flavour and amazingly vibrant colour.

1. Set aside 50 g (1¾ oz) of the custard creams for decoration. Place the remaining ones in a sandwich bag and crush with a rolling pin to get a fine crumb. Tip the crushed biscuits into a bowl and mix with the melted butter, then press the mixture into the lined cake tin.
2. In a medium bowl, whisk together the custard powder and sugar. Whisk in the cream, followed by the egg. Pour onto the custard cream base and spread out evenly.
3. Air fry at 160°C (325°F) for 17–22 minutes, until the custard is golden on top and set but still slightly soft in the centre.
4. Remove from the air fryer, cover with the rhubarb compote and allow to cool to room temperature before slicing into 9 squares. If you want a sharp cut, chill for 2–3 hours before slicing.
5. Just before serving, break the remaining custard creams into chunks and sprinkle over each square.

CINNAMON CRUMBLE CAKE

Serves	6-8
Prep time	15 minutes
Bake time	35-40 minutes

Equipment

18 cm (7 inch) round cake tin, greased and lined

For the Cake

80 g (3 oz)	unsalted butter, softened
75 g (2½ oz)	granulated sugar
1	large egg
50 g (1¾ oz)	natural yogurt
2 tablespoons	water
120 g (4 oz)	self-raising flour
¼ teaspoon	bicarbonate of soda
¼ teaspoon	fine salt

For the Filling and Topping

70 g (2½ oz)	soft light brown sugar
¾ teaspoon	ground cinnamon
30 g (1 oz)	self-raising flour
30 g (1 oz)	unsalted butter
pinch	fine salt

This moist, light cake features a ribbon of cinnamon-sugar running through its centre and is topped with a crunchy cinnamon crumble. It's based on an American-style 'coffee cake', meant to be eaten for brunch alongside a hot cup of joe (rather than containing any coffee), but we think it goes equally well with tea!

1. Make the filling first. In a small bowl, combine 20 g (¾ oz) of the brown sugar with ½ teaspoon of the cinnamon. Set aside.
2. Now make the crumble topping. Place the remaining sugar and cinnamon in a medium bowl with the flour, butter and salt. Rub together with your fingertips to get a breadcrumb-like mixture. Set aside.
3. Make the cake batter by creaming the softened butter and granulated sugar together until smooth and light. Beat in the egg, yogurt and water. Fold in the flour, bicarbonate of soda and salt to get a thick batter.
4. Spread half the cake batter into the prepared cake tin and sprinkle with the cinnamon-sugar filling. Dot the remaining cake batter on top then spread out into an even layer. Sprinkle on the crumble topping.
5. Air fry at 160°C (325°F) for 25 minutes, then reduce the setting to 150°C (300°F) and air fry for a further 10–15 minutes until browned, and a toothpick inserted into the centre of the cake comes out clean. Let cool for 10 minutes in the tin before turning out on to a wire rack, crumble side up, to cool completely.

EARL GREY & MIXED FRUIT LOAF

Makes . . . . 1 loaf cake

Prep time . . . . . 5 minutes, plus 2 hours steeping

Bake time . . . . . 45 minutes

Equipment

450 g (1 lb) loaf tin, base and sides greased and lined, foil

For the Fruit Loaf

300 ml (½ pint) . . boiling water
4. . . . . Earl Grey tea bags
100 g (3½ oz). . . . dried mixed fruit
50 g (1¾ oz) . . . . . dried mixed peel
1 . . . . lemon, finely zested and juiced
2. . . . . large eggs
150 g (5½ oz) . . . . self-raising flour
100 g (3½ oz). . . . soft light or dark brown sugar
50 g (1¾ oz) . . . . . salted butter, melted, plus extra, softened, to serve

Fragrant and citrusy, this cake is lovely and moist thanks to the long soak of the fruit. It's not too sweet so is an ideal afternoon treat, either on its own or as more of a tea bread with extra salty butter!

1. Pour the boiling water into a jug, add the tea bags, mixed fruit and peel and stir well. Leave for as long as you can, ideally overnight but at least a couple of hours.
2. When ready to bake, fish out the tea bags then pour the fruit and any remaining liquid into a mixing bowl. Add the lemon zest and juice, eggs, flour, sugar and melted butter and mix loosely to just combine. It'll be sticky and wet but that's what makes it such a moist loaf!
3. Pour into the prepared loaf tin and air fry for 20 minutes at 160°C (325°F), then cover with foil and bake for another 25 minutes.
4. Leave to cool in the tin for a couple of hours before slicing with a bread knife. This keeps really well for 3–4 days in an airtight container.

RASPBERRY CHEESECAKE ECLAIRS

Makes 6–8

Prep time . . . . . 15 minutes

Bake time . . . . . 25 minutes

Equipment

piping bag fitted with a slit nozzle, parchment or silicone liner

For the Eclairs

1 quantity . . . . . . Choux Pastry (see page 19)

100 ml (3½ fl oz). . double cream

150 g (5½ oz) . . . . cream cheese

1 teaspoon. . . . . . instant custard powder

1 teaspoon. . . . . . vanilla extract or paste

3–4 tablespoons . raspberry jam

1 . . . . digestive or ginger nut biscuit

20 g (¾ oz). . . . . . freeze-dried raspberries

These wouldn't look out of place in the window of a French patisserie, but take less than an hour to make from scratch! We make a cheat's pastry cream by adding some instant custard powder into our double cream and then add cream cheese to make it a rich cheesecake filling – heaven.

1. Follow the instructions on page 19 to make your éclairs. Depending on the size of your air fryer basket you may need to bake them in 2 batches. Poke a little hole in in the bottom to allow the steam to escape, then let them cool completely before slicing in half down the centre like a hot dog bun.
2. Add the cream, cream cheese, custard powder and vanilla to a mixing bowl and whisk to stiff peaks. Fold through your raspberry jam until you get lovely pink streaks throughout.
3. Add the cheesecake mixture to the piping bag (or cut a long slit in the corner of a sandwich bag) and pipe the filling into each éclair in a wiggly line. Crumble over the biscuit and sprinkle over some freeze-dried raspberries to serve.

GIN & TONIC TRAYBAKE

Makes . . . . 9 squares

Prep time . . . . . 20–25 minutes

Bake time . . . . . 40–45 minutes

Equipment

18 cm (7 inch) square cake tin, greased and lined

For the Base

150 g (5½ oz) . . . . butter, softened, or margarine
150 g (5½ oz) . . . . caster sugar
2. . . . . large eggs
150 g (5½ oz) . . . . self-raising flour
50 ml (2 fl oz). . . . gin
1 . . . . lime, finely zested and juiced
50 ml (2 fl oz). . . . tonic water

For the Icing

150 g (5½ oz) . . . . icing sugar
25 ml (1 fl oz) . . . . gin
½. . . . . lime, finely zested and juiced

Whatever your favourite tipple, alcohol makes bakes super fluffy, and when baking in an air fryer this makes the lightest cakes. We both love an icy G&T after a 'hard' day's baking, so we thought we'd combine the day's work with the evening's activity!

1. In a mixing bowl, cream together the butter or margarine and sugar until light and fluffy. Crack in your eggs and beat, followed by the flour, folding gently. Pour in the 50 ml (2 fl oz) gin then add the lime zest and juice and mix to combine.
2. Pour into your tin and level out. Air fry at 165°C (330°F) for 20 minutes before covering with foil and continuing to bake for 20–25 minutes or until a skewer inserted into the middle comes out clean. Leave to cool in the tin for 5 minutes before poking all over with a cocktail stick or skewer and brushing over the tonic water. Leave for 15 minutes, then turn out on to a wire rack and cool completely.
3. In a small bowl, mix together the icing sugar and gin for the icing. Add the lime juice bit by bit until you have a thick, smooth icing, then spread over your cake, letting it drip down the sides.
4. Sprinkle over your lime zest and leave to set for an hour before cutting into squares and serving. Optional iced G&T on the side!

ECLAIR RING CAKE

Serves. 4–6

Prep time . . . . . 20 minutes, plus 20 minutes cooling time

Bake time . . . . . 20 minutes

Equipment

piping bag fitted with round nozzle, baking paper

For the Cake

½ quantity. . . . . . Choux Pastry (see page 19)

50 g (1¾ oz) . . . . . plain dark chocolate, minimum 50% cocoa solids, chopped

For the Filling

200 ml (7 fl oz). . . double cream

4 teaspoons . . . . instant custard powder

1 teaspoon. . . . . . vanilla paste or extract (optional)

This choux pastry ring is filled with a cheat's crème diplomat (a mixture of whipped cream and instant custard) then topped with melted chocolate, in a nod to classic éclairs. The advantage here is that making one big ring cake takes less time than assembling individual éclairs, meaning you can entertain with ease!

1. Combine the filling ingredients in a medium bowl, whisk until the cream has thickened to soft peaks, then cover and refrigerate to chill.
2. Make the choux pastry according to the recipe on page 19 then pop it into the piping bag (or use a sandwich bag with the corner snipped off).
3. Cut a square of baking paper to line the basket of your air fryer. Draw a 15 cm (6 inch) circle onto it as a guide, flip it over and pipe the choux pastry on top in a ring shape. You may need to pipe a second ring on top of the first to use up all the pastry.
4. Air fry at 180°C (350°F) for 15 minutes until golden on top, then flip it over and air fry for a further 5 minutes to help crisp up the base.
5. Poke a few holes in the hot pastry to let any steam escape, then leave it in the switched-off air fryer with the drawer shut for 20 minutes. This allows the pastry to dry out so it won't collapse. Transfer to a wire rack and leave to cool completely before slicing in half horizontally.
6. Spoon or pipe the chilled filling evenly between the cut surfaces of your choux ring.
7. Melt the chocolate in the microwave, or in a heatproof bowl set over a pan of simmering water, making sure the base of the bowl isn't touching the water. Spoon the melted chocolate over the top of the ring and then leave to set (pop it into the refrigerator for 10 minutes to speed things up!) before serving.

BROOKIE BARS

Makes . . . . 8 bars or 9 squares

Prep time . . . . . 30 minutes

Bake time . . . . . 40 minutes

Equipment

18 cm (7 inch) square baking tin, base greased and lined

For the Cookie Layer

75 g (2½ oz) . . . . . salted butter, softened
75 g (2½ oz) . . . . . soft light brown sugar
1 teaspoon. . . . . . vanilla extract or paste
100 g (3½ oz). . . . plain flour
¼ teaspoon . . . . . bicarbonate of soda
80 g (3 oz) . . . . . . milk or dark chocolate chips

For the Brownie Layer

75 g (2½ oz) . . . . . salted butter
50 g (1¾ oz) . . . . . plain dark chocolate, 70% cocoa solids, chopped
150 g (5½ oz) . . . . soft light brown sugar
1 tablespoon . . . . unsweetened cocoa powder
40 g (1½ oz) . . . . . plain flour
1 . . . . medium egg
75 g (2½ oz) . . . . . white chocolate chips

Who doesn't love a chocolate chip cookie? Who doesn't love a brownie? Imagine these two became best mates and decided to hang out in an air fryer together... and you get Brookie Bars! Soft, gooey brownie with a crunchy cookie base - it doesn't get much better than this.

1. Start with your cookie dough base. In a large mixing bowl, beat together the butter and sugar for a minute or so. Add the vanilla and mix well. Fold through the flour and bicarbonate of soda, followed by the chocolate chips, to make a soft dough.
2. Press into the prepared tin and flatten with your fingers or the back of a spoon. Pop in the freezer for 15 minutes, or refrigerate for 30 minutes, then air fry at 160°C (325°F) for 20 minutes.
3. Meanwhile, make your brownie layer. Add the butter, chocolate and sugar to a medium heatproof and microwave-safe bowl and heat in the microwave in 45-second bursts until melted and smooth. Stir well to dissolve the sugar as best you can. (You can also do this in a small saucepan on the hob over a low heat.)
4. Leave aside to cool to room temperature for 10 minutes, then mix in the cocoa, flour and egg. Beat really well until thickened and the mixture sticks to itself. Fold through the white chocolate chips then pour over the baked cookie layer. Use a spatula to spread it out to the corners.
5. Air fry at 160°C (325°F) for 20 minutes, until shiny and baked around the edges. Leave in the tin for a couple of hours to cool, before slicing into 8 bars or 9 squares.

6

WEEKEND BAKES

If you've got a little more time on your hands, or you want to whip something up to impress your guests, this chapter has got you covered.

CUSTARD TART

Serves 8–10

Prep time . . . . . 15 minutes, plus chilling

Bake time . . . . . 1 hour 15 minutes

Equipment

18 or 20 cm (7 or 8 inch) fluted tart tin, blowtorch (optional)

For the Tarts

1 quantity . . . . . . Sweet Shortcrust Pastry (see page 18)

220 ml (7½ fl oz). . double cream

180 ml (6 fl oz) . . . whole milk

2 tablespoons . . . vanilla extract or paste, or 1 vanilla pod, split lengthways and seeds scraped

¼. . . . . whole nutmeg, plus extra for the top

6. . . . . large egg yolks

75 g (2½ oz) . . . . . caster sugar, plus extra (optional) to finish

A custard tart is a classic dessert, and we've stuck with tradition with a sprinkling of nutmeg to finish, but we've added a little modern twist by baking it in our air fryer. The fan will blow your custard all over, though, so don't forget to cover it! To take this pud to another level, sprinkle some sugar over the top and turn it into a crème brûlée tart, but don't do it too far in advance or your sugar will melt and you'll miss that crackly top.

1. Roll out the pastry to the thickness of a pound coin (3 mm/⅛ inch) and a little larger than your tin. Press it carefully into the tin, pushing into each flute. Leave a little excess pastry around the edge, but trim any large overhang. Prick the base with a fork and refrigerate for 15 minutes.
2. Line the chilled pastry case with baking paper and fill with baking beans or uncooked rice. Air fry at 160°C (325°F) for 15 minutes, then remove the baking beans or rice and baking paper and air fry for a further 10–12 minutes until lightly browned. Carefully remove the case from the basket, using a tea towel to protect your hands, and trim any remaining excess pastry using a sharp knife or a vegetable peeler. Brush out any crumbs and then pop back in the air fryer while you make your filling.
3. In a small saucepan over a medium heat, bring the cream and milk to a low simmer. Add the vanilla and grate in the nutmeg.
4. Add the egg yolks to a large bowl, and whisk with the sugar until smooth. Carefully pour in the boiling cream mixture while whisking to combine. Strain into a jug.
5. Carefully pour the custard mixture into the tart shell in the air fryer and grate over a little more nutmeg. Cover the tart carefully with the base of a 23 cm (9 inch) loose-bottomed cake tin then air fry at 150°C (300°F) for 30 minutes. Using silicone tongs, spin the tart around 180 degrees and continue to bake for 20 minutes; it should still have a little wobble but will set while it cools. Leave to cool completely in the air fryer basket until set.
6. When ready to serve, use a warmed knife to cut your tart into 8–10 slices. If you'd like to brûlée your tart, cover each slice with a thin layer of caster sugar and use a blowtorch to melt it. Add another layer of sugar and blowtorch again to make the perfect thick brûlee top!

JAM DOUGHNUTS

Makes 4

Prep time . . . . . 30 minutes, plus 3 hours resting and proving

Bake time . . . . . 20–22 minutes

Equipment

baking paper

For the Doughnuts

45 g (1½ oz) . . . . . full-fat Greek yogurt
45 g (1½ oz) . . . . . hot water
15 g (½ oz) . . . . . . unsalted butter, melted
1 . . . . large egg yolk
½ tablespoon . . . caster sugar
¼ teaspoon . . . . . fine salt
125 g (4 oz) . . . . . plain flour, plus extra for dusting
15 g (½ oz) . . . . . . instant mashed potato flakes
1 teaspoon. . . . . . fast-action dried yeast
½ teaspoon . . . . . baking powder
splash . . . . vegetable oil

For Coating and Filling

4 tablespoons. . . raspberry jam
2 tablespoons . . . melted butter
4 tablespoons. . . caster sugar

Okay, hear us out on this - using potatoes in your bread dough is a little hack for getting super-soft baked goods. The potato starch within is able to bind more water than the wheat starch in plain flour, which helps the dough remain really soft and squishy (while you can use mashed potatoes, we make life a little easier by going for instant mashed potato flakes instead). It's perfect for these baked doughnuts which we stuff with jam and roll in sugar for that classic flavour.

1. Mix the yogurt and hot water in a large bowl until smooth. Mix in the melted butter, egg yolk, sugar and salt.
2. In a separate bowl, mix the flour, potato flakes, yeast and baking powder together with a whisk until fully combined.
3. Tip the dry ingredients into the wet and mix together until you get a soft dough. Cover with a clean tea towel and leave to rest for 20 minutes so the dry ingredients can fully absorb the liquids.
4. Turn the dough out on to your work surface and knead for 8–10 minutes until smooth and stretchy, dusting the dough and your hands lightly with flour as needed to prevent it sticking.
5. Return the dough to the bowl, drizzle a little bit of vegetable oil over it and flip it over to coat. Cover with the tea towel and leave somewhere warm to rise until doubled in volume, 45–60 minutes.
6. Punch the dough down and tip out onto your work surface. Cut into 4 equal pieces and roll them into balls. Fit the air fryer with its crisper plate and line it with a square of baking paper. Place the dough balls on top, spacing them a few centimetres apart.
7. Cover the air fryer drawer with the tea towel and leave somewhere warm to rise until almost doubled in volume (20–30 minutes).
8. Uncover and air fry the doughnuts at 160°C (325°F) for 10–12 minutes until golden. Flip them over and return to the air fryer for a further 10 minutes until golden all over. Wrap the warm doughnuts in the tea towel and leave for 10 minutes so the crust can soften.
9. Use a paring knife to poke a hole into the side of each one, and fill with raspberry jam (you can use a piping bag with a long, pointed tip or a sandwich bag with the corner snipped off).
10. Brush with the melted butter, then toss them all in a bowl with the sugar to coat. Eat immediately!

COCONUT & CHOCOLATE MINI LAYER CAKES

Makes . . . . 4 cupcakes or 8 fairy cakes

Prep time . . . . . 30 minutes, plus cooling

Bake time . . . . . 15–20 minutes

Equipment

4 silicone cupcake cases (175 ml/ 6 fl oz capacity) or 8 silicone fairy cake cases (75 ml / 2½ fl oz capacity)

For the Cakes

100 g (3½ oz). . . . salted butter, softened
100 g (3½ oz). . . . caster sugar
2. . . . . medium eggs
90 ml (3 fl oz). . . . full-fat coconut milk
100 g (3½ oz). . . . self-raising flour
3 tablespoons . . . desiccated coconut, to finish

For the Ganache

100 g (3½ oz). . . . full-fat coconut milk
150 g (5½ oz) . . . . plain dark chocolate, 70% cocoa solids, finely chopped

If you're looking for something to bake that's as simple as a cupcake but somehow looks a little more fancy, try out this recipe. The cake batter is baked as cupcakes which are flipped upside down and sliced in two, giving you mini layer cakes! We've taken inspiration here from coconut-filled chocolate bars, by making a coconut milk ganache to sandwich between the cake layers, and using desiccated coconut to decorate.

1. Make the ganache by gently warming the coconut milk in a small pan until steaming. Remove from the heat and tip in the chopped chocolate, stirring a few times to combine. Leave to stand for 5 minutes so the chocolate can melt, before stirring until smooth. If you find the chocolate hasn't fully melted, stir the pan over a gentle heat for a minute or so to gently melt any remaining chunks. Set aside to cool and thicken.
2. In a mixing bowl, cream the butter and sugar together until smooth and fluffy. Beat in the eggs and coconut milk. Finally, fold in the flour until no floury patches remain.
3. Spoon the batter into the silicone cases, spreading it out to form an even layer and air fry at 160°C (325°F) for 15–20 minutes for cupcakes or 12–17 minutes for fairy cakes, until risen, golden and when a toothpick is inserted into the centre of a cake, it comes out clean. Place the cakes upside down on a wire rack to cool completely.
4. Once the cakes have cooled, remove from the liners and cut off any domed tops. Cut the cakes in half and spread some of the ganache between the layers. Place the cakes so they are upside down and frost with some more of the ganache.
5. Sprinkle with desiccated coconut and serve.

TIP

- If you want your desiccated coconut to be crispy, gently toast it in a small frying pan over a medium heat on the hob, stirring often until golden. Let it cool before using to decorate the cakes.

SUMMER BERRY MERINGUE CAKE

Serves. 6

Prep time . . . . . 15 minutes

Bake time . . . . . 35–50 minutes

Equipment

18 cm (7 inch) springform or loose-bottomed round cake tin, base and sides greased and lined

For the Meringue Cake

30 g (1 oz) . . . . . . unsalted butter, softened
95 g (3¼ oz) . . . . . caster sugar
1 . . . . large egg, separated
40 ml (1½ fl oz) . . . whole milk
50 g (1¾ oz) . . . . . self-raising flour
⅛ teaspoon . . . . . fine salt
150 ml (¼ pint) . . . double cream
100 g (3½ oz) . . . . Greek yogurt
200 g (7 oz) . . . . . mixed summer berries (we like strawberries and raspberries)

A lovely cake to make in the summertime when fresh berries are in their prime! It features a thin layer of rich sponge cake, topped with crispy, chewy meringue. A final layer of yogurty whipped cream is adorned with fruit for a light and delicious dessert.

1. Cream the butter, 45 g (1½ oz) of the sugar and the egg yolk together in a medium bowl until smooth. Stir in the milk, then the flour and salt. Spread into the prepared cake tin.
2. Air fry at 160°C (325°F) for 15–20 minutes, until lightly browned and a toothpick inserted into the centre of the cake comes out clean.
3. In a medium, clean bowl and using a handheld electric mixer, whisk the egg white until foamy. Gradually add the remaining sugar, 1 tablespoon at a time, whisking on a medium-low speed until fully incorporated. The egg white should be shiny and form stiff peaks.
4. Spread the meringue over the baked cake and return to the air fryer for 20–30 minutes, depending on how soft or crispy you like your meringue; it should be a light caramel colour and feel dry to the touch.
5. Let the cake cool for 10 minutes before removing from its tin and leaving on a wire rack to cool completely.
6. Whisk the cream in a medium bowl and, when it just starts to thicken, add the yogurt and fold together gently to combine. Spread the whipped cream mixture over the top of the cooled cake, decorate with the berries and serve immediately.

CHERRY & ALMOND STRUDEL

Serves. 6–8

Prep time . . . . . 15 minutes

Bake time . . . . . 40 minutes

Equipment

baking paper

For the Strudel

3 sheets . . . . filo pastry, defrosted if frozen

50 g (1¾ oz) . . . . . unsalted butter, melted

450 g (1 lb). . . . . . fresh or frozen cherries, pitted/defrosted

100 g (3½ oz). . . . glacé cherries, halved

50 g (1¾ oz) . . . . . caster sugar

60 g (2¼ oz). . . . . ground almonds

1 teaspoon. . . . . . almond extract

10 g (¼ oz) . . . . . . flaked almonds

20 g (¾ oz). . . . . . icing sugar, for dusting

To serve

Cream or ice cream

While an apple strudel might be the most common, we're big fans of Bakewell tart, so have used the easiest pastry of them all to wrap up our delicious filling: shop-bought filo! If you do prefer a classic filling, feel free to use the Flaky Speculoos Apple Pie filling on page 185, with or without the caramelized biscuit spread...

1. Cut each sheet of filo in half. Unroll a large sheet of baking paper and place a filo half sheet on it. Brush with melted butter, then place another half sheet on top and brush with butter, repeating until you have 6 layers. Make sure you trim it to the diagonal size of your air fryer.
2. Drain the defrosted cherries, if using, in a sieve and pat dry with kitchen paper. Add the fresh or defrosted cherries to a bowl with the glacé cherries, sugar, ground almonds and almond extract and mix well.
3. Spoon the mixture in a block near the shorter side of the pastry, leaving a 2 cm (¾ inch) gap. Use the baking paper to ease the pastry and filling over in a roll, ending with the seam on the bottom.
4. Brush the top with more butter and sprinkle with the flaked almonds. Cut the paper on each side to shorten if you need and to provide you with a little hammock to transfer the strudel to the air fryer.
5. Air fry at 160°C (325°F) for 15 minutes before using the paper hammock to carefully roll the strudel over and bake for another 15 minutes. Then turn the temperature down to 140°C (275°F) and bake for 5 minutes, bottom up, before turning the strudel the right way again for a final 5 minute bake.
6. Use your paper sling to carefully remove. Dust with icing sugar and serve immediately, in slices, with cold cream or ice cream.

CAULIFLOWER CHEESE GALETTES

Makes 8

Prep time . . . . . 30 minutes

Bake time . . . . . 8–12 minutes

For the Galettes

1 . . . . small cauliflower (400 g/14 oz prepared weight)
1 tablespoon . . . . olive oil
20 g (¾ oz). . . . . . salted butter
15 g (½ oz) . . . . . . plain flour
150 ml (¼ pint). . . milk
100 g (3½ oz). . . . mature Cheddar cheese, grated
½ tablespoon . . . wholegrain mustard
1 x 320 g (11½ oz) . sheet ready-made puff pastry or ½ quantity Rough Puff Pastry (see page 17)

Flaky pastry plus cheesy cauliflower is a guaranteed crowd pleaser. These are a little twist on cauliflower cheese, turning a much-loved side dish into a centrepiece. Serve them with a rocket salad dressed with zingy vinaigrette for a great veggie-friendly lunch.

1. Cut the cauliflower into small florets and toss with the oil. Add to the drawer of your air fryer, fitted with its crisper plate. Air fry at 180°C (350°F) for 15-20 minutes until mostly browned, then tip out of the air fryer and set aside.
2. Meanwhile, make a roux by melting the butter in a medium pan over a medium heat. Stir in the flour and cook for a minute to lightly toast. Whisk in the milk, a little at a time, until completely incorporated and smooth. Cook, stirring occasionally, until thickened.
3. Add the cheese and mustard, stir until the cheese has melted, then remove from the heat and stir through the roasted cauliflower.
4. If using homemade pastry, dust underneath and on top with flour then roll it into a rectangle around 25 x 35 cm (10 x 14 inches). If using ready-made pastry, gently unroll it.
5. Cut your pastry into 8 rectangles. Fold the edges of each rectangle inwards to form a 1 cm (½ inch) border all around each galette, pressing down on the corners so they adhere. Score the middle of each rectangle in a crosshatch pattern.
6. Place the pastry rectangles in the air fryer, in batches, on the (un-lined) crisper plate, leaving a bit of a gap between each one. Air fry at 200°C (400°F) for 5-7 minutes until golden on top and puffed up.
7. Press the middles of each galette down using the back of a spoon. Fill the cavity with a generous spoonful of the cauliflower cheese mixture, then return to the air fryer, in batches, for 3-5 minutes to caramelize. Use a metal spatula to remove the galettes from the air fryer to a wire rack, then enjoy them while still warm.

SPANAKOPITA SWIRLS

Makes 4

Prep time . . . . . 30 minutes

Bake time . . . . . 25–30 minutes

For the Swirls

2 x 260 g (9¼ oz) . bags of baby spinach
200 g (7 oz) . . . . . feta cheese, crumbled
6 . . . . spring onions, sliced into 1 cm (½ inch) lengths
1 . . . . large egg
2 teaspoons . . . . garlic granules
1 tablespoon . . . . dried oregano
4 large sheets . . . filo pastry (½ a 270 g/9½ oz) pack)
30–50 g (1–1¾ oz) olive oil

Crispy filo is filled with spinach, feta and spring onions and twisted into little coils for this picnic-friendly version of spanakopita.

1. Wilt the spinach by placing it in a large pan or bowl and covering with a kettle full of freshly boiled water. Let sit for a few minutes then drain and rinse with cold water. Squeeze as much water out of the spinach as possible then roughly chop and add to a mixing bowl.
2. Mix the crumbled feta into the spinach until well combined. Stir in the spring onions, egg, garlic granules and oregano.
3. Brush a sheet of filo pastry with olive oil then flip over so the dry side is facing up. Place a quarter of the filling in a line along a long edge of the pastry, leaving a bit of a border. Loosely roll up like a cigar then gently coil (gently is key, as it will break if you do it too tightly). Repeat with the remaining filo and spinach filling to make 4 pastries.
4. Lower the pastries into the air fryer fitted with its crisper plate (you may only be able to fit 2 in there at a time), leaving a bit of space in between them, and air fry at 180°C (350°F) for 25–30 minutes, flipping them over after 20 minutes, until golden brown all over.

TIP

- If you have any leftover filling, use it in an extra sheet of filo to make a fifth, little swirl: the perfect baker's snack!

STRAWBERRY & BASIL CREAM SWISS ROLL

Serves 4–6

Prep time . . . . . 20 minutes

Bake time . . . . . 10 minutes

Equipment

18 cm (7 inch) square cake tin, greased and lined

For the Swiss Roll

2 . . . . medium eggs

50 g (1¾ oz) . . . . . caster sugar, plus extra for dusting

50 g (1¾ oz) . . . . . plain flour

For the Filling

12 g (½ oz) . . . . . . basil leaves

175 ml (6 fl oz). . . . double cream

2 tablespoons . . . icing sugar, plus extra to serve

½ quantity. . . . . . Roasted Strawberry Compote (see page 21) or 100 g (3½ oz) strawberry jam

To serve

3 . . . . small strawberries, halved

6 . . . . small basil leaves

We all know and love the OG spiral of strawberry jam and light fluffy sponge, so we've not only proved you can make a perfect mini one in an air fryer, but given it a little grown-up twist too.

1. For the filling, use scissors to cut the basil leaves into really fine shreds. Add the cream to a small saucepan, add the basil and bring to the boil. Remove from the heat and leave to cool and infuse.
2. When cool, strain out the basil then whip the cream to soft peaks before adding the icing sugar. Whip again to stiff peaks then refrigerate until ready to use.
3. For the cake, add the eggs and sugar to a mixing bowl and whisk with an electric whisk until thick and pale, around 5–6 minutes. Fold in the flour, using a metal spoon.
4. Gently pour into the prepared cake tin and tip and rotate the tin to let the cake reach the corners - don't use a spoon or it'll burst the air bubbles! Air fry at 180°C (350°F) for 10 minutes until lightly browned.
5. While the cake is baking, lightly dampen a sheet of baking paper and scatter with caster sugar. When the cake has baked, tip it straight out carefully on to the sugared paper. Peel off the tin's lining paper and roll the cake and sugared paper up as tightly as you can. Leave to cool for an hour.
6. Unroll the cake and fill with the basil cream, saving 3 teaspoons to decorate, and the strawberry compote or jam. Re-roll the cake up carefully and pop on a serving plate with the seam side down. When ready to serve, dust with icing sugar then cut into slices. Finish each slice with ½ teaspoon of the reserved basil cream, a half strawberry and a basil leaf.

CANNED PEAR FRANGIPANE SLICE

Makes . . . . 9 squares

Prep time . . . . . 30 minutes

Bake time . . . . . 50-60 minutes

Equipment

15 or 18 cm (6 or 7 inch) square cake tin, base and sides lined with a sling of baking paper, secured with metal binder clips (see page 10)

For the Pastry Case

¼ quantity . . . . . Sweet Shortcrust Pastry (see page 18), chilled
2 tablespoons . . . raspberry jam
1 x 411 g (14 oz) . . . can pear halves in fruit juice, drained

For the Frangipane

50 g (1¾ oz) . . . . . unsalted butter, softened
50 g (1¾ oz) . . . . . soft light brown sugar
1 . . . . large egg
¼ teaspoon . . . . . fine salt
⅛ teaspoon . . . . . almond extract (optional)
50 g (1¾ oz) . . . . . ground almonds
20 g (¾ oz). . . . . . plain flour

The light fragrance of almond is a lovely match for subtly flavoured pears. Using canned fruit here cuts down on prep and means you can bake this even when pears aren't in season.

1. Grate the chilled pastry on the coarse side of a box grater into the prepared tin. Spread out the pastry shreds and press down to form an even layer that covers the whole base. Refrigerate for 30 minutes.
2. Meanwhile, make the frangipane by creaming the butter and sugar together in a medium bowl until smooth. Beat in the egg, salt and almond extract, if using. Stir in the ground almonds and flour.
3. Air fry the chilled pastry case at 160°C (325°F) for 12–15 minutes until golden and crisp. Let the pastry cool, then spread the jam over it, followed by the frangipane.
4. Cut each pear half in half and push them into the frangipane, leaving a bit of the pear exposed on the surface.
5. Air fry for 30 minutes, then lower the temperature to 150°C (300°F) and air fry for a further 10–15 minutes, until a toothpick inserted into the centre of the frangipane comes out clean.
6. Leave to cool in the tin for 10 minutes before lifting out and leaving on a wire rack to cool completely before slicing into squares.

TIRAMISU CAKE

Serves 6

Prep time . . . . . 20 minutes

Bake time . . . . . 15–20 minutes

Equipment

18 cm (7 inch) round cake tin, greased and floured

For the Cake Batter

2 . . . . large eggs
100 g (3½ oz) . . . . caster sugar
60 g (2¼ oz) . . . . . self-raising flour
pinch . . . . fine salt

For the Coffee Soak

½ tablespoon . . . instant coffee granules
2 tablespoons . . . boiling water
50 ml (2 fl oz) . . . . Marsala

For the Topping

100 ml (3½ fl oz) . . double cream
15 g (½ oz) . . . . . . caster sugar
20 ml (¾ fl oz) . . . Marsala
1 tablespoon . . . . unsweetened cocoa powder

Playing with the proportions of a tiramisu recipe resulted in this delightfully easy twist on the classic dessert. A whisked sponge is soaked with a coffee-Marsala mixture and finished with a fluffy whipped cream. The trick to a great tiramisu dessert (as Izy learned from her mum) is to go heavy on the cocoa powder dusting at the end – the bitterness cuts through the rich, sweet flavours so well.

1. Whisk the eggs and sugar using electric beaters in a medium bowl until pale, thick and fluffy, around 5 minutes. Sift in the flour with the salt and fold to combine, ensuring no floury patches remain.
2. Pour the cake batter into the prepared cake tin and air fry at 160°C (325°F) for 15–20 minutes until golden; when a toothpick is inserted into the cake, it should come out clean. Leave to cool completely in its tin.
3. Combine the instant coffee with the water in a jug, stirring until dissolved, then stir in the Marsala. Spoon this over the cooled cake.
4. In a medium bowl, whip together the cream, sugar and Marsala until thickened to soft peaks. Spread this atop the cake, then dust with the cocoa powder. Either serve now, or cover and chill until ready to serve, for up to 12 hours.

TIP

- To make this alcohol-free, just replace the Marsala with extra cooled, strong coffee.

SALTED CHOCOLATE CHIP COOKIES

Makes 8

Prep time . . . . . 10 minutes, plus 2 hours chilling

Bake time . . . . . 10-12 minutes

Equipment

foil

For the Cookies

70 g (2½ oz) . . . . . salted butter, softened
100 g (3½ oz) . . . . soft light brown sugar
2 tablespoons . . . golden syrup
125 g (4½ oz) . . . . plain flour
½ teaspoon . . . . . bicarbonate of soda
½ teaspoon . . . . . baking powder
75 g (2½ oz) . . . . . chocolate chips or chunks
25 g (1 oz). . . . . . . ready salted crisps
pinch. . . . . flaky sea salt

The favourite snack of Dom's partner Jack is a bag of ready salted crisps - followed closely by a chocolate bar. We love a sweet and salty moment, so decided to combine the two! Trust us, it works. And if you're even more mad than us, we've heard salt and vinegar shouldn't be knocked either!

1. Cream together butter and sugar in a mixing bowl until lighter. Stir in the golden syrup.
2. Sift over the flour, bicarbonate of soda and baking powder and fold in using a rubber spatula. Add the chocolate chips and crisps and fold again, carefully to not crush the crisps to dust!
3. Divide the mixture evenly into 8 and roll each piece into a ball. Refrigerate for at least 2 hours.
4. When you're ready to bake, line the crisper plate in your air fryer with a piece of foil. Add a pinch of flaky sea salt to each cookie, then, depending on the size of your air fryer, add 3 or 4 to the foil in the drawer. Air fry at 170°C (340°F) for 9-12 minutes, until golden brown around the edges.
5. Leave to harden up in the air fryer basket for 10 minutes before transferring to a wire rack to cool completely. Bake the second batch in the same way, or you can keep them unbaked in the refrigerator for up to a week.

GOLDEN SYRUP SELF-SAUCING SPONGE

Serves. 4–6

Prep time . . . . . 15 minutes

Bake time . . . . . 25–30 minutes

Equipment

15–18 cm (6–7 inch) round cake tin or baking dish (not loose-bottomed), or similar sized silicone liner/baking dish that will fit in your air fryer

For the Sponge

80 g (3 oz) . . . . . . golden syrup
50 g (1¾ oz) . . . . . salted butter, melted
50 g (1¾ oz) . . . . . soft light brown sugar
1 . . . . large egg
60 ml (2 fl oz) . . . . milk
100 g (3½ oz). . . . self-raising flour
½ teaspoon . . . . . baking powder
150 ml (¼ pint). . . boiling water

To serve

Custard or vanilla ice cream (optional)

This is the perfect pud for those days you're craving nostalgic comfort. It has the hallmarks of a golden syrup steamed sponge with the bonus of a saucier syrup underneath. Pouring boiling water over cake batter may seem bizarre, but trust us on this! The water sinks under the cake as it bakes, combining with the golden syrup for a ready-made sauce.

1. Spoon the golden syrup into the cake tin or baking dish.
2. In a medium bowl, whisk together the melted butter, sugar, egg and milk until smooth. Add the flour and baking powder then whisk until fully combined. Pour this over the golden syrup.
3. Gently pour the boiling water over the cake batter, then immediately and carefully place in the air fryer.
4. Air fry at 160°C (325°F) for 25–30 minutes until golden on top and a toothpick inserted into the centre comes out with no cake batter attached (the toothpick may look a bit wet because of the sauce at the bottom of the tin).
5. Let cool for 10 minutes before scooping into bowls and serving with custard or vanilla ice cream, if you like.

PEACH & PECAN COBBLER

Serves 2–3

Prep time . . . . . 10 minutes, plus cooling

Bake time . . . . . 30–35 minutes

Equipment

15–18 cm (6–7 inch) round baking dish or cake tin (not loose-bottomed)

For the Cobbler

1 x 411 g (14 oz) . . . can peach slices in syrup or juice
60 g (2¼ oz). . . . . self-raising flour
40 g (1½ oz) . . . . . caster sugar, plus a little extra for sprinkling
¼ teaspoon . . . . . fine salt
45 g (1½ oz) . . . . . unsalted butter, cubed
30 g (1 oz) . . . . . . pecans, roughly chopped
3 tablespoons . . . milk

Nothing can replace the comforting and familiar flavour of a canned peach. They really come into their own here, topped with a simple, fluffy cobbler batter.

1. Drain off the syrup or juice from the peach slices then add them to your baking dish or cake tin. Air fry at 160°C (325°F) for 10 minutes – this helps warm them and the dish up so the batter cooks quickly when we add it.
2. Meanwhile, place the flour, sugar and salt in a medium bowl and stir together. Add the cubed butter and rub it into the dry ingredients using your fingertips until you get a sandy mixture. Stir in the pecans.
3. Mix in the milk to get a soft dough. Dot this dough over the hot peaches in the baking dish and sprinkle with a little extra sugar.
4. Air fry for another 20–25 minutes until golden brown all over and a skewer inserted into the cobbler dough comes out clean. Carefully remove from the air fryer and allow to cool for 10 minutes before dishing up.

BURNT BASQUE CHEESECAKE

Serves. 8

Prep time . . . . . 10 minutes, plus overnight chilling

Bake time . . . . . 50–60 minutes

Equipment

15 cm (6 inch) round cake tin

For the Cheesecake

500 g (1 lb 2 oz) . . full fat cream cheese
500 ml (18 fl oz) . . double cream
200 g (7 oz) . . . . . caster sugar
4 . . . . large eggs
4 level tablespoons . . . . plain flour
2–3 tablespoons . vanilla paste

To serve

1 quantity . . . . . . Roasted Fruit Compote (see page 21; we used peach) or icing sugar and fresh berries

This needs an overnight rest but it is well worth the wait - the transformation from a loose batter into a fluffy, creamy cake is unreal. The compote is the ideal accompaniment and is the perfect thing to crack on with while you're patiently waiting for the cheesecake to be ready...

1. Cut a very large square of baking paper and carefully crinkle it into your cake tin, making sure that it comes all the way up the sides of the tin but trimming any particularly long bits so they don't flap into the cake.
2. If you have a blender, add all the ingredients to it and blend until smooth. Leave to rest for 15 minutes. Pour into the tin and then tap on the counter a couple of times to disperse air bubbles.
3. Without a blender, use a whisk to beat together the cream cheese, cream and sugar until smooth. Add the eggs a bit at a time, before whisking in the flour and vanilla. You shouldn't have to let this rest as it won't have as many air bubbles as with a blender.
4. Air fry at 180°C (350°F) for 30 minutes, then turn the tin round 180 degrees and either bake for a further 20 minutes for a creamy middle or for a further 30 minutes for a more set centre when cool.
5. When the cheesecake is dark brown on top and risen (it should still be really jiggly in the middle), remove from the air fryer and let cool to room temperature. Refrigerate overnight. Don't skip this step!
6. Use a hot knife to slice and serve with the compote, or dust with icing sugar and add some berries alongside.

GUINNESS CAKE

Makes . . . . 12 slices

Prep time . . . . . 10 minutes

Bake time . . . . . 20–25 minutes

Equipment

18 or 20 cm (7 or 8 inch) bundt tin, greased and dusted with unsweetened cocoa powder

For the Cake

175 g (6 oz). . . . . . salted butter
175 ml (6 fl oz). . . . Guinness (from a can)
2. . . . . medium eggs
100 ml (3½ fl oz). . soured cream
300 g (10½ oz). . . any sugar
50 g (1¾ oz) . . . . . unsweetened cocoa powder
150 g (5½ oz) . . . . plain flour
1 teaspoon. . . . . . bicarbonate of soda

For the Frosting

150 g (5½ oz) . . . . cream cheese
75 g (2½ oz) . . . . . icing sugar
100–150 ml (3½–5 fl oz) . . . . . double cream

A pint of the black stuff is Dom's favourite tipple at the pub, and so it follows that it also makes one of her favourite cakes! Made for countless Father's Days and birthdays, the stout makes the softest and richest chocolate sponge, which when topped with a fluffy cream cheese frosting makes every bite perfection.

1. In a pan over a medium heat, melt the butter and Guinness together. Whisk together the eggs and soured cream in a jug, until smooth.
2. In a mixing bowl, whisk together the sugar, cocoa powder, flour and bicarbonate of soda. Pour in your melted butter and Guinness and stir to mix well. Pour in your soured cream and egg mixture and whisk again until smooth.
3. Pour into the prepared tin and air fry at 160°C (325°F) for 20–25 minutes, until risen and a toothpick inserted into the cake comes out clean. Leave to cool in the tin for 10 minutes before turning out on to a wire rack to cool completely.
4. To make the frosting, beat the cream cheese in a mixing bowl until smooth. Sift in the icing sugar and mix well. Add 100 ml (3½ fl oz) cream and whisk until smooth and thickened. If you like a slightly stiffer frosting, add the remaining cream and repeat.
5. Swoosh and swoop the frosting over the lovely cooled ring. Store any leftovers in the refrigerator (although we can't guarantee there'll be any…).

TIP

- If you don't have a bundt tin, follow the basic Sponge Cake instructions on page 14 for baking in a round tin or a loaf tin.

7

ON THE GO

Picnic in the park? Lunch at your desk? Giant hike? Pack your lunchbox with delicious bakes that are easy to take on the go and won't fall apart when rattling around in a bag.

SUN-DRIED TOMATO & FETA FOCACCIA

Makes . . . . 1 loaf

Prep time . . . . . 35 minutes, plus proving

Bake time . . . . . 30–40 minutes

Equipment

18 cm (7 inch) round or square cake tin (not loose-bottomed), base and sides lined with a sling of baking paper, secured with metal binder clips (see page 10)

For the Focaccia

1 quantity . . . . . . Bread Dough (see page 16), made with olive oil, and 210 g (7½ fl oz) warm water (for a wetter dough)

75 g (2½ oz) . . . . . sun-dried tomatoes in oil, snipped with scissors into strips 1 cm (½ inch) wide

100 g (3½ oz) . . . . feta cheese, crumbled

pinch. . . . . flaky sea salt

While plain focaccia is the stuff of dreams, with its bubbly bounciness and crispy crust, we've taken it up a notch by folding in sun-dried tomatoes and crumbled feta. Eat it on its own, dipped into olive oil and balsamic, or use it to make an epic sandwich for your lunchbox.

1. Make the bread dough following the instructions on page 16, using olive oil, and increasing the amount of water.
2. Once the dough has risen, sprinkle the chopped sun-dried tomatoes and crumbled feta over the dough in the bowl. Do a couple of sets of stretch-and-folds to incorporate them into the dough.
3. Pour a tablespoon of the oil from the jar of tomatoes into the lined tin. Tip in the dough and stretch it gently to fill the tray (don't worry if it doesn't fully reach the corners as it will spread as it rises). Cover with a clean tea towel and leave somewhere warm until almost doubled in volume.
4. Once risen, deeply dimple the dough all over with your fingertips and drizzle with a final tablespoon or two of the oil from the jar of tomatoes. Sprinkle with a pinch of flaky salt.
5. Air fry at 180°C (350°F) for 20–30 minutes until deeply golden on top. Turn the focaccia out from its tin and remove the baking paper. Return it upside down to the air fryer for a further 10 minutes so the base can crisp up and get golden.
6. Let the focaccia cool on a wire rack, right side up. Once fully cooled, slice into chunks and serve.

OATY CHEESE BISCUITS

Makes 20–24

Prep time . . . . . 30 minutes

Bake time . . . . . 20 minutes

Equipment

baking paper

For the Biscuits

50 g (1¾ oz) . . . . . plain flour, plus extra for dusting
40 g (1½ oz) . . . . . porridge oats
¼ teaspoon . . . . . bicarbonate of soda
60 g (2¼ oz). . . . . cold salted butter, cubed
100 g (3½ oz). . . . mature Cheddar cheese, grated
1 teaspoon. . . . . . demerara sugar

Crumbly cheese biscuits are a great addition to a cheese board. They're topped with a little sprinkle of demerara sugar which rounds out their salty, savoury flavour.

1. In a medium bowl, combine the flour, oats and bicarbonate of soda. Add the cubed butter and rub it into the flour using your fingertips. Add the grated cheese and gently knead it into the dough by hand until cohesive.
2. Roll the dough into a long snake, around 4 cm (1½ inches) thick (using a light dusting of flour, if needed to prevent sticking). Pop into the freezer for around 10 minutes to firm up.
3. Slice the dough into 20–24 equal rounds. They may deform or crack in places when you do this, but just mould back into a circle by gently squishing them with your hands.
4. Line the basket of your air fryer with a square of baking paper and place the cheese biscuits on top, leaving a bit of space between each circle (you will likely need to bake them in batches). Sprinkle the top of each with a little demerara sugar.
5. Air fry at 160°C (325°F) for 15 minutes until golden on top, then flip them over and bake for a further 5 minutes to get the bottoms golden too. Transfer to a wire rack to cool completely before eating.

SEEDED CRACKERS

Makes	8–10
Prep time	15 minutes
Bake time	40 minutes for each batch

Equipment

18 cm (7 inch) square cake tin or baking tray, greased and lined

For the Crackers

20 g (¾ oz)	chia seeds
60 g (2¼ oz)	mixed seeds: pumpkin, sesame, poppy, sunflower, linseed
10 g (¼ oz)	fennel, cumin, nigella or caraway seeds (or a mix of all)
75 ml (2½ fl oz)	boiling water
½ teaspoon	fine sea salt
1 teaspoon	dried herbs: sage, rosemary, basil

Protein-packed and super light, these crispy, crunchy crackers are the perfect base vehicle for cheese or to dip in tzatziki or houmous.

1. Mix together all the ingredients in a small bowl and leave to stand for 15 minutes, stirring halfway.
2. Spread half the thickened paste into the prepared tin and level out with the back of a dampened spoon. Score with a knife in a grid pattern for easy breaking.
3. Air fry at 160°C (325°F) for 25 minutes, then use an offset spatula to carefully turn the cracker over and continue to bake for 15 minutes until cooked through and dry on both sides. Repeat with the remaining mixture to bake a second batch.
4. Leave to cool completely on a wire rack before breaking up and serving with cheese, soup or dips.

VEGGIE SAUSAGE & CHUTNEY ROLLS

Makes 12

Prep time . . . . . 20 minutes

Bake time . . . . . 25–30 minutes

For the Rolls

½ quantity. . . . . . Rough Puff Pastry (see page 17) or ½ x 320 g (11½ oz) ready-rolled puff pastry sheet
pinch. . . . . plain flour, for dusting (optional)
3 tablespoons . . . caramelized onion chutney
250 g (9 oz) . . . . . vegetarian sausages, defrosted if frozen
1 teaspoon. . . . . . fennel seeds
1 teaspoon. . . . . . smoked paprika
1 tablespoon . . . . black onion seeds

TIP

- You can easily double up the recipe and bake the sausage rolls in 2 batches, if you want to use up the whole pack of ready-rolled puff pastry. Otherwise, re-roll the remaining puff pastry, pop into a sandwich bag and freeze for another time.

Adding a layer of chutney in these sausage rolls brings a sticky sweetness. We add some extra spices into the sausage 'meat' to give them an extra layer of flavour which you can customize to your liking. Here, smoked paprika and fennel seeds make them taste a bit like pepperoni(!) but check out the flavour variations under the recipe for other ideas.

1. Roll the half ready-rolled pastry sheet out into a roughly 20 x 35 cm (8 x 14 inch) strip. If using homemade, dust lightly with flour and roll out into a strip roughly 20 x 35 cm (8 x 14 inches).
2. Spread the chutney down the centre of the strip of pastry.
3. Remove any casings of the sausages, if present, then add them to a medium bowl.
4. Toast the fennel seeds in a small, dry frying pan until fragrant, and add to the bowl along with the smoked paprika. Squish together by hand to mix everything well.
5. Add the filling all down the length of the pastry on top of the chutney. Fold the pastry over the filling and pinch to seal the edges together. Cut into 12 equal pieces.
6. Fit the air fryer with its crisper plate and place the sausage rolls on top, leaving a bit of space between each. Brush the tops with a little water and sprinkle with the black onion seeds.
7. Air fry at 180°C (350°F) for 25–30 minutes, until golden all over. Let them cool for 10 minutes before eating, as the chutney will be super hot straight out the air fryer!

VARIATIONS

- Add 1 teaspoon toasted, crushed cumin seeds and 1 teaspoon garam masala to the sausage 'meat' and pair with mango chutney.
- Add 1 tablespoon wholegrain mustard and the leaves from 3 sprigs thyme to the sausage 'meat', and pair with Branston pickle.

GARLIC BUTTER PULL-APART BREAD

Makes . . . . 1 loaf

Prep time . . . . . 15 minutes, plus 2–3 hours proving

Bake time . . . . . 25–30 minutes

Equipment

450 g (1 lb) loaf tin or 18 cm (7 inch) square cake tin, greased

For the Bread

250 g (9 oz) . . . . . strong white flour

5 g (⅛ oz) . . . . fast-action dried yeast

½ teaspoon . . . . . caster sugar

½ teaspoon . . . . . fine sea salt

25 g (1 oz). . . . . . . salted butter, softened (you can also use vegan butter)

150 ml (¼ pint) . . . warm milk or water

50 g (1¾ oz) . . . . . Cheddar or mozzarella cheese, grated (optional)

For the Garlic Butter

50 g (1¾ oz) . . . . . salted butter, softened

2 . . . . garlic cloves, finely grated or minced

small bunch . . . . . parsley, finely chopped

good pinch . . . . . salt

We know we've said the filling is optional, but cracking these little balls open to reveal a cheesy middle really makes this recipe a winner. We also wouldn't say no to dipping them into any remaining garlic butter, like a certain well-known pizza joint…

1. Add all the dry ingredients to a mixing bowl and mix. Add the softened butter then the liquid, slowly, stirring until no loose flour remains. Turn out on to a work surface and knead for 8–10 minutes until the dough smooths out. Pop in a greased bowl, cover with clingfilm or a damp tea towel and leave in a warm place for an hour or 2 until it has risen to double its size.
2. To make the garlic butter, use a spatula to smoosh the butter in a bowl and then add the garlic, parsley and salt. Leave at room temperature.
3. When risen, split the dough into 10 balls. If using cheese, push a pinch of it into the middle of each ball.
4. Brush each ball with some garlic butter and pop into your prepared tin, letting the balls pile up. Finish by brushing some of the extra garlic butter (keep some for later) over the bread and then cover again. Leave for another hour or so in a warm place until puffed up again.
5. Air fry at 170°C (340°F) for 15 minutes before covering with foil and baking for another 10–15 minutes.
6. When out of the oven, brush with some extra garlic butter and leave to cool for 20 minutes in the tin before removing and tearing straight in!

BUTTERNUT SQUASH, BLUE CHEESE & BROCCOLI QUICHE

Serves. 4-6

Prep time . . . . . 30 minutes

Bake time . . . . . 45-50 minutes

Equipment

18 or 20 cm (7 or 8 inch) high-sided fluted tart tin

For the Quiche

1 quantity . . . . . . Shortcrust Pastry (see page 18)

¼ small . . . . butternut squash (100 g/3½ oz)

¼ small . . . . head broccoli (100 g/3½ oz)

splash . . . . olive oil, for coating

2. . . . . large eggs

150 ml (¼ pint). . . double cream

100 ml (3½ fl oz). . crème fraîche

100 g (3½ oz). . . . blue cheese, crumbled

4 sprigs. . . . . thyme, leaves stripped

pinch. . . . . salt and pepper

Quiche is a picnic classic, and this recipe and the variation opposite are sure to please any crowd. The ingredients are totally interchangeable with whatever you have in the refrigerator, but we always love a bit of cheese in there to add a little sharpness! Depending on the height of your tart tin, you may have a little filling left over, but you can just bake that in a ramekin afterwards for 5-10 minutes until set, as a treat for yourself.

1. Roll out your pastry to the thickness of a pound coin (3 mm/⅛ inch) and a little larger than your tin. Press it carefully into the tin, pushing into each flute. Prick the base with a fork and refrigerate for 15 minutes.
2. While it's chilling, peel, deseed and roughly chop the squash, and roughly chop the broccoli. Toss with a little olive oil and a pinch each of salt and pepper, and air fry at 200°C (400°F) for 15 minutes, to part-cook, then set aside in a bowl to cool.
3. Line the chilled pastry case with baking paper and fill with baking beans or uncooked rice. Air fry at 160°C (325°F) for 15 minutes, then remove the paper and beans or rice and bake for a further 10-12 minutes until lightly browned. Check the underside of the base carefully to make sure it's cooked through.
4. In a mixing bowl, whisk together the eggs, double cream and crème fraîche before adding the blue cheese and thyme leaves and mixing through your partly cooked squash and broccoli.
5. Tip the filling mixture into the pastry case and air fry at 160°C (325°F) for 20-24 minutes, until cooked through. There still may be a small wobble in the centre, but it will continue to set as it cools. Leave to cool in the tin for 30-40 minutes before either serving straight away with a green salad, or leaving to cool completely and taking with you.

CHORIZO, RED PEPPER & POTATO QUICHE

Serves 4–6

Prep time . . . . . 30 minutes

Bake time . . . . . 45–50 minutes

Equipment

18 or 20 cm (7 or 8 inch) high-sided fluted tart tin, silicone liner

For the Quiche

1 quantity . . . . . . Shortcrust Pastry (see page 18)
100 g (3½ oz). . . . cooking chorizo
1 small jar. . . . . . . red peppers (185 g/6½ oz drained weight), or 1 fresh red pepper
½ can. . . . . peeled new potatoes (100 g/3½ oz drained weight)
2 large. . . . . eggs
150 ml (¼ pint). . . double cream
100 ml (3½ fl oz). . crème fraîche
small bunch. . . . . flat leaf parsley, finely chopped
100 g (3½ oz). . . . mature Cheddar cheese, grated

1. Roll out your pastry to the thickness of a pound coin (3 mm/⅛ inch) and a little larger than your tin. Press it carefully into the tin, pushing into each flute. Prick the base with a fork and refrigerate for 15 minutes.
2. While it's chilling, crumble or roughly chop the chorizo and add to a silicone air fryer liner. Air fry at 180°C (350°F) for 5 minutes before removing to a bowl. Roughly chop the drained jarred or fresh red pepper and the canned potatoes, then add to the chorizo.
3. Line the chilled pastry case with baking paper and fill with baking beans or uncooked rice. Air fry at 160°C (325°F) for 15 minutes, then remove the beans or rice and baking paper, and bake for a further 10–12 minutes until the base is lightly browned. Check the underside of the base carefully to make sure it's cooked through.
4. In a mixing bowl, whisk together the eggs, double cream and crème fraîche before adding in your chorizo mixture and parsley, along with a good pinch each of salt and pepper. Fold through the grated cheese.
5. Pour into the part baked pastry case and then air fry at 160°C (325°F) for 20–24 minutes until cooked through. There still may be a small wobble in the centre, but it will continue to set as it cools. Leave to cool in the tin for 30–40 minutes before serving. Or leave to cool completely before taking with you.

SAVOURY ANTIPASTO SWIRLY BUNS

Makes 6

Prep time . . . . . 15 minutes, plus 1 hour proving

Bake time . . . . . 20 minutes

Equipment

6 large (175 ml/6 fl oz) silicone muffin cases

For the Buns

1 quantity . . . . . . Bread Dough (see page 16)
4. . . . . artichoke pieces from a jar
2. . . . . roasted peppers from a jar
2. . . . . pickled chillies from a jar
50 g (1¾ oz) . . . . . pitted olives
100 g (3½ oz). . . . Manchego cheese, grated
8 slices . . . . salami (optional)
1 . . . . egg, beaten
pinch. . . . . salt and pepper

Aperitivo at sunset and a game of Uno are some of Dom's best holiday memories - always accompanied by some delicious snacky bits. These buns are all the best bits of an antipasto board, squished into a focaccia-style dough, which makes them the ideal pairing with a cold beer or spritz!

1. Make your dough following the instructions on page 16, until the beginning of its first rise. While it's rising, make your filling.
2. Drain your artichokes, peppers, chillies and olives well, and dab with kitchen paper to remove a little more of the oil. Chop everything roughly together, to make a paste. Season with salt and pepper and set aside.
3. When your dough is ready, knock it back and then roll out to a rectangle 35 x 25 cm (14 x 10 inches). Spread the antipasto paste over the dough then sprinkle over the cheese. If using salami, lay the slices along a short side, overlapping slightly.
4. Roll the dough up tightly from a short side, then cut into 6 pieces. Place each piece swirly side up in a muffin case and brush with beaten egg. Let rise again in a warm place, covered with clingfilm, for an hour or until doubled in size.
5. Just before baking, brush with some more beaten egg and air fry at 160°C (325°F) for 20 minutes until risen and golden.
6. Leave to cool for 15 minutes before enjoying, or let cool completely and pack up for an on-the-move snack!

KIMCHEESE SCONES

Makes 4

Prep time . . . . . 10 minutes, plus chilling

Bake time . . . . . 25 minutes

For the Scones

275 g (9¾ oz) . . . . self-raising flour
1 teaspoon. . . . . . baking powder
½ teaspoon . . . . . bicarbonate of soda
60 g (2¼ oz). . . . . cold salted butter
175 g (6 oz). . . . . . extra-mature Cheddar cheese, grated
200 g (7 oz) . . . . . kimchi
50–75 ml . . . . milk (2–2½ fl oz)

Our favourite place to catch up is in a café over a toastie, and kimcheese is one of the best flavours out there at the moment. These are great straight out of the air fryer, eaten with some salty butter while the cheese is still melty, but if you're enjoying them later on a picnic, they're just as good on their own.

1. Sift the flour, baking powder and bicarbonate of soda into a bowl. Grate your chilled butter in the flour mixture then rub between your fingertips lightly until the mixture reaches a breadcrumb texture. Fold the grated cheese through, using a knife.
2. Pop your kimchi on a chopping board with a lip and roughly chop. Using gloves if you prefer, squeeze the liquid from the kimchi into a measuring jug with your hands (try to squeeze as much out as you can).
3. Add the chopped kimchi to your flour and cheese mixture and fold through. Add the milk to the kimchi liquid to make up to 125 ml (4 fl oz) in total. Slowly pour your kimchi milk a bit at a time into the flour mixture, to bring the dough together. Don't add too much – you want it to just come together without being sticky.
4. Pat your dough into a square that's just smaller than your air fryer drawer. Cut diagonally into 4 triangles and refrigerate for 5–10 minutes to firm up slightly.
5. Add your scones to the air fryer, directly on the crisper plate, and bake for 20 minutes, until golden, before flipping them over carefully and baking for another 5 minutes.

OPINEL

CHEESE & OLIVE TWISTS

Makes	15 large or 30 mini twists
Prep time	20 minutes
Bake time	20 minutes

For the Twists

1 quantity	Rough Puff Pastry (see page 17)
100 g (3½ oz)	mature Cheddar or other strong cheese, grated
100 g (3½ oz)	Parmesan cheese, grated
200 g (7 oz)	pitted mixed olives, chopped
small handful	thyme sprigs, leaves picked

We've added olives as our 'twist' on the classic cheesy number but you can add all sorts - try sun-dried tomatoes, artichokes or even mixed chopped nuts. They keep really well for 3-4 days, and 2 minutes in the air fryer again refreshes them wonderfully. You can also bake them from frozen, with the same timings as below.

1. Make the pastry following the instructions on page 17. On your final turn, scatter over the grated cheeses, chopped olives and thyme leaves.
2. Turn over and press the fillings in well. Roll out to a large rectangle, around 30 x 20 cm (12 x 8 inches) and use a pizza cutter to slice into strips - long or short, you decide. Twist them over themselves, lay onto a plate or tray and place in the refrigerator while you finish preparing the remaining twists.
3. You'll need to bake these in batches, but they take the same baking time whether they're long wiggly ones or short mini twists! Add them to the crisper plate and air fry at 160°C (325°F) for 15 minutes, then use tongs to turn them over and bake for another 5 minutes until golden brown on both sides.

YOGURT POT MUFFINS

Makes . . . . 6 muffins or 9 fairy cakes

Prep time . . . . . 10 minutes

Bake time . . . . . 15–25 minutes

Equipment

6 silicone muffin cases (175 ml/6 fl oz capacity) or 9 silicone fairy cake cases (75 ml/6 fl oz capacity)

For the Muffins

1 pot (110–120 g/3¾–4 oz) . . . . natural yogurt
1 pot . . . . granulated sugar
1 . . . . large egg
½ pot. . . . . vegetable oil
2 pots . . . . self-raising flour
pinch . . . . fine salt
½ teaspoon . . . . . ground cinnamon or 1 orange/lemon, finely zested

This is a great recipe to memorize in case you ever want to bake but don't have kitchen scales to hand. The idea is to use a yogurt pot to measure all your ingredients for a quick and simple batter that you can stir together in no time. We like to use natural yogurt but you can go for fruited versions if you want an extra hit of flavour.

1. In a medium bowl, whisk together the yogurt, sugar, egg and oil until the batter is smooth.
2. Add the flour, salt and cinnamon (or orange/lemon zest) then fold together to get a thick batter.
3. Divide the mixture between the silicone muffin or fairy cake cases.
4. Air fry at 160°C (325°F) for 20–25 minutes if making muffins, or 15–20 minutes for smaller cakes, until golden, and when a toothpick inserted into the centre of a muffin comes out clean.
5. Remove the muffins to a wire rack to cool completely.

NEW YORK COOKIES

Makes . . . . 6 large cookies

Prep time . . . . . 15 minutes

Bake time . . . . . 17–20 minutes

Equipment

baking paper or parchment liner

For the Cookies

60 g (2¼ oz) . . . . . unsalted butter, softened
60 g (2¼ oz) . . . . . granulated sugar
60 g (2¼ oz) . . . . . soft light brown sugar
1 . . . . large egg
2 teaspoons . . . . vanilla extract
½ teaspoon . . . . . fine salt
145 g (5 oz) . . . . . plain flour
½ teaspoon . . . . . baking powder
½ teaspoon . . . . . bicarbonate of soda
200 g (7 oz) . . . . . mixed chocolate chips
100 g (3½ oz) . . . . chopped nuts, such as hazelnuts, walnuts, pecans

These are inspired by the famous Levain bakery based in NYC, whose cookies are HUGE and packed full of mix-ins. You can bake the cookies as soon as you make the dough, but our favourite option is to bake two fresh, chill two balls of dough to bake later in the week, and freeze the last two for whenever a craving hits.

1. Cream the butter and sugars together in a medium bowl until smooth, then mix in the egg, vanilla and salt. Add the flour, baking powder and bicarbonate of soda, and stir together to get a soft dough. Finally, mix in the chocolate chips and chopped nuts.
2. Divide into 6 equal balls (around 100 g/3½ oz each). Place 2 or 3 balls of cookie dough (depending on how many can fit) in the air fryer fitted with its crisper plate and lined with baking paper, spacing them a few centimetres apart to allow room for then to spread.
3. Air fry at 160°C (325°F) for 15 minutes until golden and puffy, then turn the setting down to 150°C (300°F) and finish them off for a further 2–5 minutes until the edges are set but the middles are soft.
4. Let the cookies cool on the baking paper for a few minutes before using a metal spatula to transfer them to a wire rack to cool fully.
5. Either cook the rest of the cookie dough balls in the same way or place them in a sealed container and store in the refrigerator for up to 7 days, or freeze for up to 3 months. When ready to eat, simply air fry 1 or 2 balls of cookie dough as outlined above (no need to defrost), flattening them slightly on a piece of baking paper and giving them an extra 2 minutes for the main bake.

WHITE CHOCOLATE BROWNIES

Makes 9

Prep time . . . . . 10 minutes

Bake time . . . . . 40–45 minutes

Equipment

18 cm (7 inch) square cake tin, base and sides lined with a sling of baking paper (see page 10) or with a silicone liner

For the Brownies

150 g (5½ oz) . . . . white chocolate, chopped
125g (4½ oz) . . . . unsalted butter
150 g (5½ oz) . . . . caster sugar
100 g (3½ oz). . . . plain flour
¼ teaspoon . . . . . fine salt
2. . . . . large eggs, beaten
1 tablespoon . . . . vanilla extract or paste
Handful. . . . . freeze-dried raspberries (optional)
150 g (5½ oz) . . . . white chocolate chips

A blondie this is not! Squidgy and fudgy with four perfect corner pieces – the best words to describe a brownie. Here, we're leaning into the lighter notes of white chocolate with a vanilla-spiked batter and some sharp raspberries to balance the flavour.

1. In a heatproof and microwave-proof bowl, microwave the chopped white chocolate with the butter in 45-second bursts, until melted and smooth. Leave the mixture to cool for a few minutes.
2. Add the sugar and stir, followed by the flour and salt. Add the egg a little at a time, and mix well until smooth. Stir through the vanilla and, if you're using the freeze-dried raspberries, fold them in here.
3. Pour the batter into the prepared tin and scatter over the white chocolate chips (make sure to poke any raspberries down or they'll burn).
4. Air fry at 160°C (325°F) for 20 minutes, then cover with foil and bake for another 20–25 minutes until golden brown. They may still be a bit wobbly in the centre but will set up when cooled. Leave to cool completely in the tin – this is a must to retain their fudginess! Slice into 9 squares to serve.

FLAKY SPECULOOS APPLE PIES

Makes 4

Prep time . . . . . 45 minutes, plus chilling

Bake time . . . . . 32–35 minutes

Equipment

parchment or silicone liner

For the Apple Pies

1 quantity . . . . . . Rough Puff Pastry (see page 17)
2 tablespoons . . . unsalted butter
2 . . . . green apples (Bramley or Granny Smith, around 400 g (14 oz) total weight, peeled, cored and diced
½ teaspoon . . . . . cornflour mixed with 1½ teaspoons water
4 tablespoons . . . caramelized biscuit spread, such as Biscoff (crunchy or smooth) or 50 g (1¾ oz) caster sugar
1 teaspoon. . . . . . ground cinnamon
1 . . . . medium egg
2 tablespoons . . . demerara sugar

Once you've got your rough puff pastry down, the possibilities for fillings really are endless. We've gone with the viral sensation of caramelized biscuit spread paired with sharp, tangy apples, but berries or even tropical fruits would be equally good. These are delicious warm, straight out of the air fryer, but hold up surprisingly well in an airtight container for al fresco desserts... squirty cream welcomed.

1. Start by making your rough puff pastry following the instructions on page 17. After your last turn, roll out to a rectangle 30 x 20 cm (12 x 8 inches), the thickness of a pound coin (3 mm/⅛ inch). Refrigerate while you make your filling.
2. Melt the butter in a small saucepan, add the apples and cook down for 5 minutes until softening at the edges. Add the cornflour mix and the caramelized biscuit spread (or sugar if you're not a speculoos fan). Cook for 3–4 minutes until the mixture has thickened slightly, then stir through the cinnamon and leave to cool completely.
3. Cut your pastry into 4 large squares and spoon a quarter of the filling onto one half of each.
4. Beat the egg and brush around 3 of the edges of each square. Fold over the pastry to encase the apple filling and press down the edge with a fork. Brush the tops with egg and sprinkle each with the demerara sugar. Make a couple of slits in the centre of each and refrigerate for 30 minutes.
5. Add to the air fryer on its crisper plate in a silicone or parchment liner and air fry at 160°C (325°F) for 20 minutes until golden brown on the top. Flip over and bake for a further 12–15 minutes until baked on the bottom.

CHOCOLATE ORANGE BABKA

Serves 8

Prep time . . . . . 15 minutes, plus 2 hours proving

Bake time . . . . . 25–30 minutes

Equipment

450 g (1 lb) loaf tin, buttered and floured

For the Babka

200 g (7 oz) . . . . . strong white flour, plus extra for dusting
5 g (⅛ oz) . . . . fast-action dried yeast
2 teaspoons . . . . sugar (any)
½ teaspoon . . . . . salt
50 g (1¾ oz) . . . . . unsalted butter, softened
1 . . . . large egg, beaten
50 ml (2 fl oz) . . . . warm milk
1 . . . . large orange, zested

For the Filling

25 g (1 oz). . . . . . . soft light brown sugar
50 g (1¾ oz) . . . . . unsalted butter
50 g (1¾ oz) . . . . . milk or plain dark chocolate, roughly chopped
20 g (¾ oz). . . . . . unsweetened cocoa powder
1 . . . . large orange, finely zested

For the Glaze

100 g (3½ oz). . . . icing sugar
1 . . . . orange, juiced

Chocolate and orange has to be one of the best combinations out there, so we thought why not roll it into a sweet, rich dough and cover it in a sharp citrus glaze? This cake is delicious served as part of a brunch spread as well as an afternoon tea, so if you'd like to bake it in the morning, you can do your second prove (after braiding) in the refrigerator overnight instead.

1. Start by making your filling. Add the sugar, butter, chocolate and cocoa powder to a small heatproof and microwave-safe bowl. Microwave in 45-second bursts until the chocolate is melted and smooth. You can also do this on the hob over a low heat in a small pan. Pop in the refrigerator to cool to a paste while you make your dough.
2. Add the dough ingredients to a large mixing bowl and mix to combine. Tip out on to a floured surface and knead well for 5–6 minutes until a smooth dough is formed. Add a bit more flour and then roll out to a rectangle, 30 x 20 cm (12 x 8 inches), the thickness of pound coin (3 mm/⅛ inch). Spread your cooled filling over the dough evenly with the back of a spoon and sprinkle over the orange zest.
3. Starting from a long side, roll the dough tightly into a Swiss roll. Slice down the middle lengthways to make 2 long pieces.
4. Squish the 2 ends together at one end, then braid the 2 long pieces of dough together, twisting in a spiral shape. Squish the other ends together and tuck the whole thing into your prepared loaf tin, joined ends underneath. Cover and leave in a warm place for 2 hours until well risen or doubled in size.
5. Air fry at 160°C (325°F) for 25–30 minutes until risen and golden. Leave to cool in the tin for 30 minutes before turning out onto a wire rack.
6. For the glaze, combine the icing sugar and orange juice in a bowl and either pour over the completely cooled babka, or brush it on. Leave to set for an hour before slicing and serving – or take the whole thing with you and tear into it as you go!

GLOSSARY OF UK/US TERMS

Ingredients

All ingredients are as stated in the recipe. It is important to weigh ingredients for accuracy as is always the case in baking, but particularly for these recipes as they are generally small-batch bakes and so the margin for error is smaller. For example, egg sizes must be used as stated (medium and large) as the liquid in a larger egg might make your mixes too runny and not bake correctly.

Standard level spoon measurements are used in all recipes.
1 tablespoon = one 15 ml spoon
1 teaspoon = one 5 ml spoon
Both Imperial and metric measurements have been given in all recipes. Use one set of measurements only and not a mixture of both.
Eggs should be medium unless otherwise stated.

Please note: UK and US egg sizes are different. This book has been tested with UK egg sizes, which are larger than US egg sizes.
1 UK medium egg = 53–63 g/ 2 oz
UK large egg = US extra-large egg

baking beans . . . . pie weights
bicarbonate of soda . . . . baking soda
biscuit . . . . cookie
cake tin . . . . cake pan
caster sugar . . . . superfine sugar
clingfilm . . . . plastic wrap
condensed milk . . . . sweetened condensed milk
cornflour . . . . cornstarch
demerara sugar . . . . turbinado sugar
desiccated coconut . . . . dried, shredded, unsweetened coconut
digestives . . . . graham crackers
double cream . . . . heavy cream
icing . . . . frosting
filo pastry . . . . phyllo dough
flaked almonds . . . . slivered almonds
foil . . . . aluminum foil
ginger nut . . . . ginger snap
glacé cherries . . . . candied cherries
ground almonds . . . . almond flour
icing sugar . . . . confectioners' sugar
jug . . . . pitcher
mature Cheddar . . . . sharp Cheddar
pepper . . . . bell pepper
piping bag . . . . pastry bag
plain flour . . . . all-purpose flour
porridge oats . . . . oatmeal
rocket . . . . arugula
self-raising flour . . . . self-rising flour
spring onions . . . . scallions
sultanas . . . . golden raisins
vanilla pod . . . . vanilla bean
wholemeal flour . . . . wholewheat flour

INDEX

Authors' Acknowledgements

We had such a great time creating this book, and while we had each other to bounce ideas off, lots of great people helped us along the way. We'd like to offer our thanks and appreciation to them.

To Izzy Jessop, for believing in our vision and guiding us through the process. To Jonathan Christie, for his amazing design work that captured our personalities and recipes perfectly. To Alex Stetter, for her diligent eye, and to Caroline Alberti, for turning this into an actual book.

We'd wanted to shoot a book together for so long, and it was made even more fun by the on-set team: Lucy Cottle and Eden Owen-Jones smashed it in the kitchen, and Barnaby Radford-Wilson brought fantastic energy and captured some of our most special moments.

Finally, we'd like to thank our long-suffering chief recipe tasters, Jack and Andy, who have supported us for many years and given us vital feedback on all elements when asked (and also when not!).

First published in Great Britain in 2025 by Hamlyn, an imprint of Octopus Publishing Group Ltd
Carmelite House
50 Victoria Embankment
London EC4Y 0DZ
www.octopusbooks.co.uk

An Hachette UK Company
www.hachette.co.uk

The authorised representative in the EEA is Hachette Ireland, 8 Castlecourt Centre, Castleknock Road, Castleknock, Dublin 15, D15 YF6A, Ireland

Distributed in the US by
Hachette Book Group
1290 Avenue of the Americas
4th and 5th Floors
New York, NY 10104

Distributed in Canada by
Canadian Manda Group
664 Annette St.
Toronto, Ontario, Canada M6S 2C8

ISBN 978-0-60063-902-2

A CIP catalogue record for this book is available from the British Library.

Printed and bound in China.

10 9 8 7 6 5 4 3 2 1

Junior Commissioning Editor: Isabel Jessop
Senior Editor: Alex Stetter
Creative Director: Jonathan Christie
Photography: Isobel Hossack
Food styling: Dominique Eloïse Alexander
Prop styling: Dominique Eloïse Alexander & Isobel Hossack
Production Manager: Caroline Alberti